Season On The Line

This is a work of fiction. All of the characters, events, and organizations portrayed in this work are either products of the authors' imagination or used fictitiously.

Season On The Line
Copyright © 2014 by Shawn Pfautsch

All rights reserved. No part of this book may be reproduced in any form by any electronic or mechanical means including photocopying, recording, or information storage and retrieval without permission in writing from the author.

ISBN-13: 978-0692317716
ISBN-10: 0692317716

Cover art by Delicious Design League

For information about production rights, contact:
seasononthelineplay@gmail.com

Published by Sordelet Ink

Season On The Line

A PLAY BY
Shawn Pfautsch

Published by
Sordelet Ink

SEASON ON THE LINE received its world premiere on September 24th, 2014 by the House Theatre of Chicago. It was directed by Jess McLeod. Set and Lighting Design by Lee Keenan, Sound Design by Kevin O'Donnell, Costume Design by Izumi Inaba. The production was stage managed by Brian DesGranges.

The cast was as follows:

ISH: Ty Olwin
BEN ADONA: Thomas J. Cox
DAY STARR: Maggie Kettering
NAN TUCCI: Allison Latta
ELIZABETH FRICKE: Marika Mashburn
PETER TRELLIS: Andy Lutz
KAKU WADU: Danny Bernardo
MICKEY NDWADDEEWAZIBWA: Abu Ansari
JOHN GREEN: Marvin Quijada
AMOS DELANEY: Shane Kenyon
FAYE: Tiffany Yvonne Cox
JOAO: Christopher Walsh
VALERIE DENT: Jessica Dean Turner
ASHLEY SALT: Mary Hollis Inboden
SYDNEY SMITHE: Bob Kruse
ARTHUR WILLIAMSON: Sean Sinitski
ENSEMBLE: Molly Lyons, Rawson Vint

Cast of Characters

THE NARRATOR - A KIND OF ISHMAEL*

BEN ADONA - ARTISTIC DIRECTOR OF *BAD SETTLEMENT THEATRE COMPANY*

DAY STARR - STAGE MANAGER FOR *BSTC*

NAN TUCCI - ASSOCIATE ARTISTIC DIRECTOR, CASTING DIRECTOR, ACTOR, INSOMNIAC

ELIZABETH FRICKE - DIRECTOR OF *GATSBY*, ANN IN *BALM*, STUBB IN *MOBY DICK*

PETER TRELLIS - TOM IN *GATSBY*, DIRECTOR OF *BALM*, FLASK IN *MOBY DICK*

KAKUEMON (KAKU) WADA - DANCER, SINGER, ACTOR, QUEEQUEG

MUWANGI (MICKEY) NDWDADDEEWAZIBWA - UGANDAN-ENGLISH ACTOR AND DRAMATURG

JOHN GREEN - MAKAH INDIAN, AN ACTOR AND SOUND DESIGNER

AMOS DELANEY - COMPANY MEMBER EMERITUS, BACK FROM LA, PLAYING JOE AND ISHMAEL

FAYE AWEE - AUTHOR OF *ATTAINABLE FELICITY: MELVILLE AND BAHA'I*

JOAO - A WHALER FROM THE AZORES, TECHNICAL DIRECTOR

VALERIE DENT - A COSTUME DESIGNER, NEW TO THE ROOM

ASHLEY SALT - A TERMINALLY MID-LEVEL LIGHTING DESIGNER

SYDNEY SMITHE - SET DESIGNER, SELF-DESCRIBED

JONAS CLAY - AUDITIONING

ARTHUR WILLIAMSON - THEATRE CRITIC FOR *THE TIMES*

---

* THE CHARACTER OF THE NARRATOR IS CALLED *ISH* IN THE SCRIPT — THIS IS NOT THE NAME OF THE CHARACTER, BUT A CONVENIENT PLACEHOLDER. THE CHARACTER SHOULD BE LISTED AS "THE NARRATOR" IN THE PROGRAM, NOT "ISH".

ACT I

Ish 1 - Incantation

ISH
Lights... go.

Why are you here tonight?

Are you looking to be moved? Entertained? Did you read a good review, I hope?

What were your expectations? Right before I started talking, what did you want, more than anything, for the next three hours to be about?

I come here to be entertained. I come here to be moved. But the best times I've had at a theatre were not because I left thinking about how much I loved it. My favorite nights are not the ones where I left talking about a great actor, or a stunning set, or how tight the pacing was, or how clear the direction, or how well the stage manager called it. My favorite nights in the theatre are the ones where I left asking questions, maybe getting into an argument - not about whether the show was good or not, but whether we are good or not. Or if childhood is better than adulthood. Or whether honesty is the same thing as truth.

Those are my expectations. The thing is - I didn't start out with those expectations. Neither did you. We accrued them like scars and other wisdoms. But we have them and now we have to deal with them. You have them. You have them. You definitely have them.

When I first showed up in a theatre - the pool room of the former Constellation Motel, inhabited by Bad Settlement Theatre Company - I had no expectations about entertainment, catharsis, pacing, ticket sales... critics... I answered a want ad for an Assistant Stage Manager. I showed up like a wolf-child at the door, with no idea what language these people were speaking.

Oh. My name... is in the program. You don't have to look now. It'll be there.

Scene 1 - This is a Theatre

(ISH enters the Board Room. A flurry of activity. The production meeting is being set up. DAY is sitting at the table engrossed in a report she is writing)

ISH
Hi, I'm looking for Day?

DAY
In the flesh. You must be my new ASM. Nice to meet you.

ISH
Likewise.

DAY
This is your orientation packet. Don't open it now.

ISH
What do I do?

DAY
Just sit next to me. *(to everyone)* Welcome to the first production meeting for Moby Dick.

(applause) I know that most of us know each other, but let's go around the room and introduce ourselves because that's what people who like each other do. Liz, would you like to start?

ELIZABETH
E-lizabeth Fricke, assistant director. I'm also directing a little play called The Great Gatsby to which you are all invited to rehearsal after this.

NAN
Nan Tucci, casting director, associate artistic director.

JOHN
John Green, sound designer... composer, question mark?

DAY
We don't need any scoring... as far as we know.

JOHN
I won't take any vacations, just in case.

ASHLEY
Ashley Salt, Lights.

JOAO
Joao. Whaling instructor. Technical Director.

VAL
Valerie Dent, Costume designer.

SYDNEY
Sydney Smythe, set designer.

MICKEY
Mickey Ndwaddeewazibwa, Dramaturgy.

DAY
Day Starr, Stage Manager, ad hoc Production Manager. Welcome, everyone, especially to our new ASM and Val. God knows we need some fresh faces around here. Ben trusts that all of you have recently finished a read-through of the book.

(Everyone pulls out their heavy, dog-eared and labelled copies of Moby Dick)

DAY
Are there any questions--

VAL
I'm sorry... so Ben Adonna is directing this play... yes?

(Everyone else is tickled by this)

ELIZABETH
He's in a Nesting Phase.

DAY
He's in his room, working on the script. He'll be calling in to the meeting later.

VAL
Oh, okay.

DAY
Any more questions?

ELIZABETH
Ishmael? Question mark?

DAY
Nan, is there a casting update?

NAN
It's not final, but now that his series is over, Ben has made an offer to Amos-

JOHN
Amos is coming back?! Holy shit! That's huge!

NAN
I can already hear the ticket lines ringing.

DAY
He is pretty.

ELIZABETH
He's too pretty. I don't believe it when a pretty person says smart things.

NAN
You weren't complaining about how pretty he was when you cast him as Hamlet, Liz.

ELIZABETH
E-Lizabeth. Hamlet is pretty and dumb, but Ishmael needs to disappear. Amos is incapable of not being looked at.

NAN
Well Ben and I and the season ticket holders think it's a great idea. But Amos's manager won't let him accept Ishmael unless we also offer him Joe in Balm In Gilead.

ELIZABETH
Does Peter know? *(Nan shakes her head)* Can I tell him?

DAY
And on that note...

(DAY gets a call on her phone. She picks up)

DAY
Yes. Hold on a second. I'll put you on speaker.

BEN
Hello, Room of Sages.

EVERYONE
Hello, Ben/Hello/Howdy *(etc.)*

BEN
I wish I could be there, but I'm in the middle of an unusually productive period and I want to take advantage of it. I can tell you that the first two acts are finished and that I'm uncommonly proud of them.

Our Moby-Dick is a memory play - not historical fiction. Ishmael is a survivor, one that has dealt with survivor's guilt, anger, and post-traumatic stress disorder. But this is not a memory that Ishmael is presenting to us to save himself, he is already saved. Ishmael is saving the lost spirits of his comrades and by extension, us.

MICKEY
Saving us from what, Ben?

BEN
Exactly. The answer is in Gatsby, in Balm in Gilead, in the newspapers this morning, in Us - we are all experiencing post-traumatic stress disorder from the loss of the American Dream... How does that sound?

JOHN
Okay, so the soundtrack to imagination is... white noise - the sound of the space. So for Ishmael, it would be his memory of the sound of the sea. What if, in his quest to get to the heart of the ocean, to the heart of our recovery, he gets to the heart of the sound, so we go from the wind and

waves to the sound of one wave in the ocean to the sound of one atom in that wave?

ASHLEY
What if the entire show were one long fade, like a three hour count from warm New Bedford to Davy Jones Locker. I know that's impossible, but I feel like we're talking about a show that doesn't have hard edges, you know? And I think that feeds into what John is saying about focus. Maybe we even play with tightening the iris on the space itself - like big warm washes at the beginning and we keep ratcheting down until we're just a special on Ishmael.

VAL
Ben, I'm really excited about the idea of the memory of a costume...

BEN
Okay. Who is that?

VAL
Val?

DAY
Valerie Dent?

BEN
Yes. Welcome aboard, Valerie.

VAL
Thank you-

BEN
So, the memory of a costume?

VAL
Yes. Now, this world, each of these sailors might have gone to the same general store for their

clothes and bought the same outfit. And over time, each crew member would have made this basic outfit their own. Stubb might have made a special pocket for his pipe; the carpenter may have ripped off his sleeves, I don't know. But maybe there's an opportunity with Ishmael to see his new clothes go through that process-

BEN
What I love about your approach, Val, is that it makes sense. But I think there's a more organic way into Ishmael's imagination.

VAL
Oh.

BEN
Use your gut.

VAL
Okay.

BEN
Don't worry, Val. The Room of Sages exists to help each other get to a deeper level of honesty and imagination.

SYDNEY
I'm sorry, while you were talking I sketched this idea.

DAY
Can I see?

SYDNEY
The Greek stage is the root of theatre the same way this book is the root of American art. That's too big for verisimilitude. So it's just a bare platform cantilevered out over the old pool so that

it appears to be floating and behind it are these looming shapes that suggest both sails and whale bones.

BEN
That's the heart of a memory play - it's too big for verisimilitude. What if we rip this down to the studs? We have this simple floating platform, the idea of costumes, perhaps the props are all mimed. But... at the very end as Ishmael delivers the epilogue, we roll the deck away and we see him floating in the old pool on a real coffin, floating with harpoons, rope, pieces of boat and whale, floating in the reality of our broken dreams.

NAN
I'd say that's pretty fucking inspiring. Can I start the capital campaign for the new building?

JOHN
Broadway, here we come.

DAY
Joao, what would it take to retract this platform twenty feet?

JOAO
About... forty feet.

DAY
How much room do we have?

JOAO
About... fifteen. It would be easier to fly like a drawbridge.

DAY
Would the grid be able to carry that?

JOAO
No. But also, the pool leaks. If this was in the budget for the season, we could have done it. Now...

BEN
So if we want this to be idea, we'll need to move fast?

JOAO
I suppose...

BEN
Good. Joao, call me later and we'll discuss. Day, make me a copy of Sydney's sketch. All right everyone, good first meeting. I need to get back to act three. Casting off. Thank you everyone.

(Ben hangs up)

DAY
All right. Presentations in two months. I'd like to commend our new ASM on a successful first production meeting.

ISH
I didn't say anything.

DAY
Keep up the good work. *(laughter)* Meeting adjourned!

(Everyone begins to pack up)

DAY
Joao, come meet the new ASM.

JOAO
You have experience with screw guns?

ISH
Yeah, I can... I can screw. Things. Together.

JOAO
He is very... *(he makes a simple, unreadable gesture)*

DAY
We should be going.

ISH
Nice to meet you! Day, what does *(gesture)* mean?

(DAY leads ISH out of the Board Room)

DAY
You'd have to ask Ben. I am untrained in Azorean gestures. I think *(gesture)* means "smile". If it doesn't, he's a very bad man. So what theatre company did you say you worked at last?

ISH
I didn't.

DAY
Well, don't leave me hanging.

ISH
No, I never have. Worked in a theatre.

DAY
You've never ASM'd?

ISH
Nope.

(entering the theatre)

DAY
Great. This is a theatre.

Ish 2 - Manilla Folder

(a special on the manilla folder in ISH's hand. Maybe DAY uses a flashlight to spot it while she smokes a cig)

ISH
Lights. Go.

The contents of a manilla folder embossed with my name in permanent marker and festooned with a Bad Settlement Theatre Company sticker, handed to me in the previous scene by Day, my new manager.

First: the obligatory packet of government mandated employment forms, all paper-clipped together with a one-inch Regal Owl clip. Fancy.

Second: a black-and-white photocopy of a photocopy of the Bad Settlement Theatre Company Mission Statement. On company letterhead. "From the desk of Ben Adonna: Bad Settlement Theatre Company strives to transform audiences with back-bending, deeply-probing, athletic honesty that engages the imagination, soul and intellect to leave the world a more fertile place for future generations.

Third: A full-color Bad Settlement Theatre Company season brochure. "Now in its 20th season of soul-searching original work, Bad Settlement Theatre Company strikes through the mask of the American Dream to investigate its Golden Age, perversions and the hope of its rebirth. Bad Settlement Theatre Company strives to show its audience that the quest for the American Dream is the quest for the American Soul with three all new productions: The Great Gatsby (new adaptation by resident enfant terrible Elizabeth Fricke); a new look at a new American classic, Balm in Gilead by Lanford Wilson (directed by Bad Settlement favorite, Peter Trellis) and concluding with artistic director Ben Adonna's new revelatory adaptation of the quintessential American novel: Moby Dick. "One of America's premier cultural institutions" (Arthur Williamson, The Times, 1998) turns 20 with a powerful message of exuberance, failure and ultimately: transformation. Don't miss our most powerful season yet.

Light and sound - go.

Scene 2 - Is This Racist?

(A rehearsal for The Great Gatsby. DAY and ELIZABETH sit at the production table, ISH beside them. The cast is in a rehearsal hotel suite. They are all wearing rehearsal pajamas. NICK is being played by a large stuffed bear. KAKU/DAISY and the BEARY GRANT/NICK are dancing to jazz music from outside)

PETER *(as TOM)*
Old sport... Did you pick that up in Oxford?

JOHN *(as GATSBY)*
Not exactly.

PETER *(as TOM)*
I understand you went there. Oxford.

ELIZABETH
Turn downstage.

JOHN *(as GATSBY)*
Yes -- I went there.

PETER *(as TOM)*
I'd like to know when.

JOHN *(as GATSBY)*
It was 1919. I only stayed five months. That's why I can't really call myself an Oxford man. It.... uh... line.

DAY
It was an opportunity-

JOHN *(as GATSBY)*
It was an opportunity they gave to some of the officers after the Armistice. We could go to any of the universities in England or France.

(There is a knock at the door)

KAKU *(as DAISY)*
Come in.

NAN *(as JORDAN)*
Unless you know what's good for you...

MICKEY *(as WAITER)*
(knocking and entering) Room service.

KAKU *(as DAISY)*
Open the whiskey, Tom, and I'll make you a mint julep. Then you won't feel so stupid... Look at the mint!

PETER *(as TOM)*
Wait a minute. I want to ask Mr. Gatsby one more question.

JOHN *(as GATSBY)*
Go on.

PETER *(as TOM)*
What kind of row are you trying to cause in my house anyhow?

KAKU *(as DAISY)*
He isn't causing a row. You're causing a row. Please have a little self-control.

PETER *(as TOM)*
Self-control! I suppose the latest thing is to sit back and let Mr. Nobody from Nowhere make love to your wife. Well, if that's the idea you can count me out... Nowadays people begin sneering at family life and family institutions, and next they'll throw everything overboard and have intermarriage between black and white.

NAN *(as JORDAN)*
We're all white here.

(Everyone looks at the waiter)

ELIZABETH
Hold! *(to ISH)* Is this racist?

ISH
Hm?

ELIZABETH
Is this racist? I'm seriously asking: is this racist? You don't have to worry about hurting my feelings - I don't have any.

ISH
Kind of?

ELIZABETH
I've totally ruined this play. You guys are awesome. This is all going to be awesome. Let's all get in a circle. Everybody take a seat on the floor.

NAN
Should we get our scripts?

ELIZABETH
Oh my god yes. Let's all get our clean, crisp white scripts out of our swarthy, racist hiding places and meet back here in a nice multiracial pow-wow. Alright people, let's get to work. Our play is kind of racist.

ISH
I didn't mean-

ELIZABETH
No. No. It is kind of racist. This is a huge problem... for a play that's supposed to be really, really racist. Thank you for honesty, noob. It is appreciated. But if this isn't really, really racist, why else are we here, dressed up for a pajama party for the American Dream where some people have nightmares because of racism?

ISH
Is that...? Are you... are you asking me... Again?

MICKEY
I have something. When I was teaching conflict resolution in South Africa, there were three words we worked to define: Racism, Discrimination and Stereotype. First - Stereotypes are beliefs about people based on their community, such as: all British people have bad teeth. Discrimination is making decisions based on those stereotypes. Australians are all noisy drunks (stereotype), therefore I will not serve this Australian gentleman a drink for fear he will start a row (discrimination). Finally, Racism is institutionalized discrimination based upon racial stereotypes. For instance -- black-colored people are dirty, stupid, sub-human animals (racial stereo-

type) therefore they can't use the same restrooms as whites (discrimination) and let's pass a law in our province making that punishable by whipping (racism). My point is that right now I see some stereotypes and some light discrimination in our production, but I don't see any racism getting in the way of the American Dream.

PETER
Because the only person who has anything specifically taken away from them is Gatsby?

(a Singularity forms on stage)

ISH
There are singularities in our lives when everything gets sucked into a moment - nothing can escape it. Everything we are is distilled into the quintessence of identity -- a tiny perfect Now...

JOHN
What if Gatsby were black?

ISH
Vapors of thought collide and congeal until their cores ignite --

KAKU
What if Daisy were white...

ISH
And then --- poof! We inflate into a new universe, with new physics.

ELIZABETH
And what if my mind exploded because you just fixed the play. Can we all agree that this is super duper racist? *(Everyone agrees)* Can we try Mickey reading Gatsby, Nan reading Daisy,

John read Nick, and Kaku read Jordan And Peter continue being racist. Is everyone cool with that?

DAY
We'll need to revisit some contracts and let Val know that costumes--

ELIZABETH
For now.

DAY
For now.

ELIZABETH
Good, because I just got goose bumps! Look--

JOHN
What about Beary Grant?

ELIZABETH
He's cut.

NAN
Who's going to read the Waiter?

DAY
(to ISH) Say "I'll read it in".

ISH
I'll read it in.

ELIZABETH
Great, noob's on it. Thanks, noob.

JOHN
On our feet?

ELIZABETH
Yes! Go go go! Unbumping!

(DAY gets a call)

DAY
It's Ben.

ELIZABETH
(to the cast) It's Ben. Whenever you're ready...

(NAN/DAISY and MICKEY/GATSBY start to dance)

PETER *(as TOM)*
Old sport. Old sport. Old. Sport. Did you pick that up in Oxford?

MICKEY *(as GATSBY)*
Not exactly, Old Sport

PETER *(as TOM)*
I understand you went there. Oxford.

MICKEY *(as GATSBY)*
Yes -- I went there.

PETER *(as TOM)*
I'd like to know when.

MICKEY *(as GATSBY)*
It was 1919. I only stayed five months. That's why I can't really call myself an Oxford man. It was an opportunity they gave to some of the officers after the Armistice. We could go to any of the universities in England or France.

(There is a knock at the door)

NAN *(as DAISY)*
Come in.

KAKU *(as JORDAN)*
Unless you know what's good for you...

ISH *(as WAITER)*
Room service.

NAN *(as DAISY)*
Open the whiskey, Tom, and I'll make you a mint julep. Then you won't feel so stupid... Look at the mint!

PETER *(as TOM)*
Wait a minute. I want to ask Mr. Gatsby one more question.

MICKEY *(as GATSBY)*
Go on.

PETER *(as TOM)*
What kind of row are you trying to cause in my house anyhow?

NAN *(as DAISY)*
He isn't causing a row. You're causing a row. Please have a little self-control.

PETER *(as TOM)*
Self-control! I suppose the latest thing is to sit back and let Mr. Nobody from Nowhere make love to your wife. Well, if that's the idea you can count me out... Nowadays people begin sneering at family life and family institutions, and next they'll throw everything overboard and have intermarriage between black and white.

KAKU *(as JORDAN)*
We're all white here.

(Everyone looks at MICKEY)

ELIZABETH
Ahhhhhhhhh! It's genius! Everybody get a pencil--

DAY
(re-entering) Five minutes, everyone.

ELIZABETH
Seriously?

DAY
That's five.

ELIZABETH
That's five.

DAY
Can I talk to you? Over here?

ELIZABETH
Day, I'm unbumping--

DAY
That was Ben. He's decided to roll all the set budgets together.

ELIZABETH
Uh huh...

DAY
And that means that we'll only be building one set for the entire season.

ELIZABETH
Come again?

DAY
And that set will be the Moby Dick set.

ELIZABETH
The floating platform thing from this morning that Sydney was using as a suppository?

DAY
We knew there would be concessions to the

budget--

ELIZABETH
My set started building today.

DAY
It did not. Ben amended your order before it was delivered.

ELIZABETH
My bouncy castle?

DAY
We'll pour one out for it at opening.

ELIZABETH
Great! Then why don't we roll all the budgets together - we'll do one play and call it The Great Dick Balm.

DAY
Elizabeth--

ELIZABETH
Peter!

DAY
Liz-

PETER
What's up?

ELIZABETH
It seems that grand poobah has decreed that we only get one set for the whole season--

PETER
What?

ELIZABETH
And guess what? It isn't an expressionist El

Greco nightmare awesome bouncy castle bed, or a gritty chrome and formica diner. It's the Moby Dick set.

PETER
What is it?

ELIZABETH
It's a retractable cantilevered platform.

PETER
Is he in his room?

DAY
He's in a Nesting Phase. The door's locked–

PETER
Great. We'll see how locked it is--

DAY
He's already cancelled your orders and reallocated the funds.

PETER
Really?

ELIZABETH
Mm-hm.

PETER
Can I have some plates and glasses?

DAY
Anything we already have in storage. I will personally find whatever either of you want.

ELIZABETH
Can we be back?

DAY
And we're back!

ELIZABETH
All right, people, hold on to your hats cuz things just got a whole lot more interesting-

ISH
All these particulars proceed from the crushing infinity of the Moment -- these moments where we Create...

SCENE 3 - THE BAR

(The actors leave rehearsal. DAY and ELIZABETH stay behind to talk)

DAY
And that's time!

ELIZABETH
Good. Rehearsal. Gatsby!

DAY
Elizabeth? The Butler-Child?

ELIZABETH
Right. If anyone knows an eight-year-old whose parents trust their child with actors, give their number to Nan. First round of drinks on Diabetes!

DAY
We need to--

ELIZABETH
Second round of drinks on Diabetes!

KAKU
Are you coming with us?

ISH
...these moments when we bond... *(to KAKU)* Me?

(He looks to DAY)

KAKU
Day?

DAY
He's coming.

ISH
... these moments directly followed with a trip to the nearest bar...

KAKU
Hello, I'm Kaku and I'll be your bartender for the evening. You're the new ASM and you look very cute taking notes. It's very co-ed.

ISH
Thanks?

KAKU
Oh, don't mind me, I'm all talk. Welcome to Bad Settlement. When did you start?

ISH
Today?

KAKU
Don't you just love Day? She is, in fact, the greatest. We like to tell her that all the time because it makes her very, very uncomfortable. Alright, what'll you have? No. Don't tell me. You...

PETER
Kaku! I'm thirsty!

NAN
Shhh! He's doing it.

KAKU
Oh mighty spirit of spirits, high lord of high balls and temple of shirleys... show me your swizzle and tipple my nipples... make my mortal orifices you own. Show me your whiskey business, all your bitters, your 'schlagers and lagers reveal to me, that I may serve this poor soul your rich bounty. You... are a beer drinker. Microbrewer, I name you. Here are our five offerings: Mog's Head, New Gallows Thief, Turpentine IPA, Street Hood Purple and Dragon Tongue Stout. You will have... Street Hood Purple.

ISH
I've never...

KAKU
Imbibe. Tell them...

ISH
This is amazing.

EVERYONE
Yay!

PETER / NAN / MICKEY
He did it! / Kaku, you're my hero! / We are not worthy!

KAKU
John, fancy bourbon. Nan, an oaky California wine. Peter, two fingers of irish whiskey. Mickey, warm ale.

ISH
And you?

KAKU
Street Hood Purple. I like beer: it's an excuse to work out tomorrow. But once I'm tipsy, tequila all the way to dawn. To a new, more racist Gatsby!

EVERYONE
To Gatsby!

ISH
What about Day?

KAKU
Day? The cheapest beer we have.

DAY
Thanks, Kaku. Bottoms up.

JOHN
Day's here!

KAKU
Day is the greatest!

DAY
Stop it.

NAN
To Day!

EVERYONE
Day!

DAY
All right. Just wait until you all start getting line notes.

KAKU
And now Day needs her fix, in 3, 2, 1--

DAY
Does anyone have a cigarette?

JOHN
I gotcha.

DAY
Just one.

JOHN
Yep, just one pack... Come on, you.

(They head outside)

ISH
That's amazing. You're like the Party Whisperer.

KAKU
It's a little thing I do. What's your thing? What's your super power?

ISH
I don't really have one.

KAKU
P-shaw. P-fooey. Everyone has one. For instance, Elizabeth's is making everything about her--

ELIZABETH
(entering) Oh my god, why are you are still here! You all have day jobs and so many new lines to learn! This is why I stopped drinking! Ah! See you tomorrow! *(She leaves)*

ISH
What does she mean by day jobs? Why do you need day jobs?

KAKU
Because money.

ISH
Aren't you all getting paid to do the show?

KAKU
Oh, you're a baby. I love that. Sweetie, nearly everyone here has another job. John bartends and works at a daycare in the morning. Nan is the Associate Artistic Director, Fundraiser-in-Chief, Interim Marketing Director, and Resident Insomniac. Mickey is a standardized patient at a teaching hospital.

MICKEY
Ow, my spleen!

KAKU
Peter, tell us about your day jobs.

PETER
Buh. Photography, personal training, the odd voice over, I used to cater. Now I need another drink.

ISH
What about Elizabeth?

PETER
Heheh. Ask her about diabetes.

KAKU
She did a commercial. She played Diabetes.

(MICKEY does an impression of ELIZABETH playing Diabetes)

PETER
You see, noob, once in a great while an actor wins the actors' lottery and gets to live off the fat teat of corporate America's obsession with the effectiveness of marketing. Wait, what did you think actors did for money?

ISH
...Act?

PETER
Oh. Oh ho ho ho. No. No no no. Oh that's... so depressing.

ISH
What about you, Kaku, are you-

KAKU
An actor? Sigh. Yes. Blegh. I hate saying that. I hate actors.

ISH
Really? Then why do you do it?

KAKU
Actors? I try not to, but they're all I ever meet.

ISH
Sorry, I don't know how any of this works.

KAKU
And that's why the spirit of spirits put you here - for me to guide you. Ask me anything.

ISH
Okay. What happened to the last ASM?

KAKU
She didn't work out.

PETER
She was Elizabeth'ed.

KAKU
Don't be dramatic.

PETER
She got totally Frick'ed.

ISH
Do people not like Elizabeth?

KAKU
No! Everyone loves Elizabeth.

PETER
So Elizabeth's first job here was directing Hamlet. And the guy playing Hamlet--

ISH
Oh! Amos?

PETER
Yes... Amos. She had Amos holding Beary Grant the entire show and give all his soliloquies to him. Honestly, it worked. I don't know why, but it did. Amos hated it, but he was too much of a wimp to say anything about it. So for weeks she told him not to do "To be or not to be" to the bear. And then one day after a run she was like "Amos, why didn't you give "to be or not to be" to Beary Grant? And he loses it. Elizabeth just listens quietly and when he's done, she says "So, you're gonna do it?" And Amos says "sure thing, Queen 8-year-old". The thing is: we'd been calling her that for weeks behind her back and he just comes out and says it. Cuz he's an idiot. And she laughed and laughed in that way she does and told him he should call her "Queen 8-year-old" for the rest of rehearsal. So he did. And he started to kill it. Just kill it. It was like being able to make fun of her in the room fixed the play. First preview rolls around, and from the moment Amos stepped on stage until the curtain call, the other actors wouldn't refer to him, on stage,

in character, as anything other than Whiney Baby Poopy Pants. When he got off stage he went storming up to Elizabeth yelling "How dare you do that to me" but Elizabeth just calmly pulled out the programs for the show and said "I don't know know why you're so upset, the programs are right: "Whiney Baby Poopy Pants" by William Shakespeare, starring Widdle Miss Diaper Rash."

ISH
And after all that, Amos wants to come back?

PETER
Amos is coming back? Why? For what? Where did you hear that? Nan?

NAN
I don't know where he heard it...

ISH
At the meeting earlier. Today.

NAN
The confidential production meeting? That one?

ISH
Was I not supposed to...

PETER
Nan, what's Amos coming back for?

NAN
Peter, shut up and listen: it's not decided yet but Ben wants him for Ishmael.

PETER
I knew it! I fucking knew it!

NAN
But he won't play Ishmael unless we also cast him as Joe in Balm in Gilead.

PETER
Really....

NAN
For the record, Amos would make a great Joe.

PETER
For the record, you looooove him.

NAN
For the record, I am a professional.

PETER
For the record, it's my show and I can cast whoever I want.

NAN
For the record: No.

PETER
Really? For the record - I quit. Sayonara, assholes.

ISH
Did he just quit?

(JOHN and DAY re-enter)

JOHN
See you tomorrow, Peter.

PETER
No you won't. I quit.

KAKU
Peter? Oh, he quits twice a week.

DAY
See you tomorrow, Peter.

KAKU
And then everyone has an excuse…

NAN, JOHN, MICKEY and DAY
I think it's time I went home.

KAKU
What about you?

ISH
I'll have another.

KAKU
Me, too.

Scene 4 - Bali Hai

ISH
The night wore on, the tequila came out and we went exploring. At some point Kaku and I and a bottle of tequila stumbled into the theatre... I'm in a theatre!!!

KAKU
This used to be the pool room. Ben did a version of South Pacific a couple years ago, it was the last play Ben directed - I was Bloody Mary - Bali Haiiiiii may call you any niiiight any day... Anyhoo, we filled the pool and had water ballets and water fights. Oh and there were no seats! That's right! That's why no one came. Well, that and the reviews.

ISH
What is this?

KAKU
A Cheseborough.

ISH
A What?!

KAKU
A Cheseborough. It connects things. What's your super power? You never told me.

ISH
What's this?

KAKU
A Gobo. Stop changing the subject…

ISH
This?

KAKU
Duvetyne. I can do this all night.

ISH
This?

KAKU
Block and tackle.

ISH
I'll block and tackle you!

(They wrestle. KAKU gets the upper hand)

KAKU
What. Is. Your. Super power?

ISH
My super power…

(A loud noise in the hall, like someone dropped a very heavy sword)

ISH
… is distraction! Take that, you gobo!

(Another loud noise)

KAKU
Sh!

(Third loud noise. Suddenly BEN is in the theatre, holding a harpoon)

BEN
"One often hears of writers that rise and swell with their subject, though it may seem but an ordinary one. How, then, with me, writing of this Leviathan? Unconsciously my chirography expands into placard capitals. Give me a condor's quill! Give me Vesuvius' crater for an inkstand! Such, and so magnifying, is the virtue of a large and liberal theme! We expand to its bulk. To produce a mighty book, you must choose a mighty theme."

The whale has expanded in Ishmael's mind to become his mind. In this theatre, we are in his memory, therefore we are in the whale. In Gatsby, we chase the whale. In Balm, we battle and lose to him. Here we pass into the guts of him - the great free creature of our souls made manifest in the melting pot of the American Experiment. We pass into his guts and are tested by him and only Ishmael and the audience fight their way back out again. How do we do that?

(He is gone)

KAKU
Oh my god. Oh my god. Oh my god.

ISH
Was that Ben? I should go meet him.

KAKU
No no no no. I'm going to make you one more drink. It's called a Preemptive Strike.

ISH
Oh ho ho. What's that?

KAKU
It's a shot of water in a pint of water. With a two aspirin chaser.

ISH
Boo!

KAKU
I'm the Drunk Whisperer. Come with me.

ISH
Distraction!

KAKU
Come on, superboy...

Scene 5 - Old Sport

ISH
Preemptive Strike. You're all welcome to have that one. A headache remedy from Kaku to me to you. Speaking of heads, Gatsby was charging ahead. The set had been rebuilt...

(lights up on SYDNEY and JOAO)

SYDNEY
I don't understand why we're four days behind. I gave my assistant the drawings to deliver two days early.

JOAO
Two days before build is not two days early.

SYDNEY
And we re-built the platform with the correct base. Lights maybe lost half a day of cue-ing.

JOAO
I've never met this assistant. *(gestures)*

ISH
The lights re-focused...

(lights up on ASHLEY)

ASHLEY
Waiting on Sydney? Ha. Every time I light a Sydney set, I build into my tech schedule what I like to call "Sydney Saturday" where I watch him have a meltdown trying to figure out why his Franken-set isn't working. You know, like the one that a poor TD tried to build based on Sydney's elevations which were drawn on napkins delivered by nineteen-year-old boys in the middle of the night. All the while I sit back, eat all the tech snacks and take notes for my memoirs, tentatively titled - "Off the Grid - the Plots and Specials of a Terminally Mid-level Lighting Designer". I also considered "What the Gel?!"... you know, like "WHA?!". Eh.

JOAO
(entering) We had to lower the platform six inches.

ASHLEY
And there's another chapter. You can't write this shit!

ISH
The costumes were tweaked...

(Lights up on ELIZABETH and VAL. PETER parades in full football pads)

ELIZABETH
Haha! Oh my god! You look so stupid! He looks so stupid!

VAL
Do you hate it?

ELIZABETH
I love it! Can the pads be, like, twice as big? Like ridiculous big?

VAL
Uh, sure. That's a more modern silhouette--

ELIZABETH
Yes, fine. And when we get his shoes, can they have those... what do you call them, the spikes?

VAL
Cleats?

ELIZABETH
Yes! Cleats! Who's next? More more more!

VAL
Peter, why don't you go change? You can spit the mouthguard out now.

(KAKU enters as Mrs. Wilson)

ELIZABETH
AH! You're hideous! Look at your fan! And your hair! What is that thing?

VAL
Which thing?

ELIZABETH
The thing?

VAL
The obi?

ELIZABETH
It's horrible! Isn't it horrible? Can you breathe?

VAL
We can change--

ELIZABETH
Change? Are you kidding? It's perfect! I hate it!

ISH
And the sound... did it's... sound thing.

(lights up on DAY at her table. JOHN comes rushing off stage in costume)

JOHN
Hold please.

DAY
Hold for sound.

JOHN
Loud noise!

(small noise. VAL enters and fits an indian headdress on JOHN)

DAY
Keep holding?

(JOHN taps at his computer)

JOHN
One secoooooooond... Loud noise!

(slightly louder noise)

JOHN
The hell? Joao!?

DAY
Okay, while we're stopped--

(deafening noise)

JOHN
Got it!

ISH
And previews were upon us. One moment you're having the first reading, the next moment, you're getting ready to go on stage in front of a lot of people with expectations. None the least being: the Critic of Note. At this time, the object of our attention, the great blank slate of terror was a man by the name of Arthur Williamson. Even during previews, the locker talk started.

JOHN
Is Arthur coming tonight?

MICKEY
It's a preview.

JOHN
So? When has that ever stopped him.

NAN
He told me he was coming opening night.

JOHN
So? When has that ever stopped him.

ISH
… and continued into the next day….

PETER
Is Arthur coming tonight?

NAN
No.

JOHN
Did I hear Arthur's coming tonight?

NAN
No! He's not coming tonight. He wouldn't have a ticket.

PETER
Arthur doesn't have a ticket?

NAN
Stop it. He's coming opening night.

ISH
... and before the last preview...

JOHN
So... Arthur. Coming tonight?

NAN
No. Opening.

KAKU
He's done it before.

JOHN
See!

MICKEY
He's inconsistent.

JOHN
He's evil.

ELIZABETH
Are you guys talking about Arthur?

JOHN
I believe you heard the word "evil? Who else would we be discussing?

NAN
He's not evil.

ELIZABETH
I don't want that job. Most people are angry at you for one review or another so they won't talk to you, and the one's that do probably want some-

thing from you. And newspapers are dying.

NAN
And he's been very good to this company so don't be ungrateful.

JOHN
I'm not ungrateful. I think he's right most of the time. I just think... he's political, he plays favorites, he gives passes to certain companies--

NAN
That is just not true.

JOHN
It is. But most of all, he just sits there with his head in his notepad not enjoying himself.

ELIZABETH
Aha! That's what this is about. That poor man does have to be political - everyone knows who he is - so everyone's watching him for a reaction which you shouldn't be watching him for anyway!

MICKEY
Arthur is more dependent on us making good shows than we are on him writing good reviews.

JOHN
And don't you think he knows it.

ISH
Which brings us to opening night... Nan?

NAN
I stood in the lobby with a press packet for twenty minutes. Because I don't have enough jobs already. Twenty minutes of me and my half-done hair,

looking like a crazy, art-deco bridesmaid, greeting donors, board members, directors, critics... "Hi Nan, is everything okay?" "Yes... just waiting for Arthur. Have a great time tonight! Ha ha, not crazy!" I'm trying to remember everybody's names while I'm trying to remember my lines.

Curtain was at 8. It was 8:15. That's par for the course on opening night but Arthur was nowhere to be seen. And Elizabeth came running out of the theatre.

ELIZABETH
What are you doing out here?

NAN
Press Packet and I are waiting for Arthur. What's that Press Packet? I look like I escaped from an opium den in 1920's San Francisco. Fuck you, Press Packet.

ELIZABETH
Sweetie -- Arthur's in the theatre.

NAN
No he isn't.

ELIZABETH
For, like, thirty minutes.

(pause)

NAN
Fantastic. Press Packet, meet your new mommy. I have to get ready.

ELIZABETH
Oooh. You should probably deliver that. I have real bad barf breath.

NAN
Great. Tell Day to hold another five for me.

ELIZABETH
I'll be here if you need me!

ISH
This was my little dominion of props and quick changes - fuzzy dice, a tomahawk, footballs. There were eighty props in my control alone. Ten quick changes. Between Day in my ear over headset--

DAY
(over headset) Okay. Let's get this party started. Lights 2 and House Out, Go.

ISH
--and a parade of actors, I was never left wanting for something to distract me from my job - which I knew very little about in the first place. As Gatsby, Mickey wasn't in the first part of the show, so he spent the first few scenes warming up.

MICKEY
Ma may mi may ma mo moo mo maaaaaaaa! Old. Old Sport. Luh. Luh. Luh-vuhl. Louis-ville. Looie-ville. Luha-vuhl. How do you say that? Can you say that for me?

ISH
Louisville?

MICKEY
Thank you. Louisville.

ISH
How do you know how it's going?

MICKEY
Mm?

ISH
How do you think it's going? Does he like it?

MICKEY
Arthur? Who knows. Arthur doesn't engage in theatre, he writes about it. And besides, Elizabeth doesn't make plays that illicit traditional enjoyment. So, there's no use worrying about it. All I can do is be in the moment, hopefully create experiences on stage for my scene partners all while trying to get this American dialect right. If the result is that the audience enjoys it, good on us. A critic gives us a good notice -- I'm sorry: review -- all the better.

ISH
Aren't you on soon?

MICKEY
I am.

ISH
Shouldn't you--

MICKEY
It's fine.

ISH
It's almost your cue line.

MICKEY
I know.

(MICKEY finishes a stretch and heads towards the door)

ISH
Good luck.

MICKEY
Break a leg?

ISH
Thank you.

MICKEY
Peter's quick change is coming up.

ISH
Oh shit.

MICKEY
(entering the stage) Your face is familiar. Weren't you in the Third Division during the War?

(PETER comes rushing in with his football uniform coming off: he dumps things on the floor as ISH quick-changes him)

ISH
How's it going?

PETER
I dropped a line in the first scene, but Kaku picked it up--

ISH
Legs.

PETER
There's a hum in the upstage right speaker that's tickling my dark desires to murder countless innocents--

ISH
Arms.

PETER
And Arthur is sitting there like he's suffering from hemorrhoids.

ISH
Head.

PETER
But now I'm about to go steal focus, so everything's aces in my book.

ISH
Your machete!

PETER
Right. *(PETER finishes his quick change, maybe by putting on a giant ridiculous mask)* Enter Crazy Party Goer Number One. Woo! *(entering)* Trimalchio! *(He exits into the theatre)*

(ELIZABETH enters from the bathroom)

ISH
Aren't you watching the play?

ELIZABETH
This play? I've seen it like thirty times.

ISH
You're not worried about how it's going?

ELIZABETH
No, it's almost over.

ISH
It just started.

ELIZABETH
Yeah, like an hour and a half ago.

ISH
Seriously?

ELIZABETH
Seriously. Welcome to backstage, noob. Things move fast.

ISH
I guess.

ELIZABETH
I'd be more worried about the quick change and gun handoff you're about to have.

ISH
Oh. Shit.

(KAKU runs off as JORDAN. ISH quick changes him into WILSON)

KAKU
Phew. Where's my martini, mister? Hello, Elizabeth.

ELIZABETH
Have you been working out?

KAKU
Yeah, working on cars all day in my greasy roadhouse really gets me all sweaty. *(he hocks a loogie)* Where's my pistol?

ISH
Right here, it's loaded. Three in the chamber.

KAKU
You're alright, son. Keep it up. *(KAKU exits into the theatre)*

ELIZABETH
That's why I'm not worried.

ISH
What about Arthur?

ELIZABETH
Arthur loves me. Even if he gives the show a bad review, he'll give me a pull-quote like "wonderfully zany" or "insightfully unconventional" or something. One time he called me "the best thing since felt" -- I think it was a compliment. It's all about context. He's been great for my career.

(ELIZABETH exits, as NAN, MICKEY and JOHN enter from the stage)

JOHN
Phew. One more, one more. We got this.

DAY
(on ISH's headset) Nobody panic, but we've got a situation down in the dressing room: the child wrangler has just informed me that little Marco has wet himself and will be unable to perform his duties as Butler in the next scene on account of the uncontrollable crying. I'm entertaining all solutions.

ISH
Oh. Oh no.

NAN
What's up?

ISH
No Marco.

JOHN
No Marco at all?

(ISH nods)

NAN
Shit.

JOHN
This is why I don't work with kids.

NAN
You work in a day-care.

JOHN
I mean, professionally. You know what I mean...

MICKEY
Where's the butler costume from act one?

ISH
It's right here.

NAN
Does anyone know the lines?

MICKEY
I can't play the butler - I'd be having a scene with myself.

NAN
I can't do it. Boobs.

DAY
(on ISH's walkie talkie) So, there's a butler in the next scene...

MICKEY
(pointing at ISH) Well, then he's got to do it.

ISH
Me?

NAN
You. Repeat after me.

(JOHN opens the door to the theatre)

KAKU
(as WILSON, on stage) Oh my god! Oh my god!

JOHN
(checking in) Scene's almost over...

NAN
"I'm going to drain the pool today Mr. Gatsby."
Focus.

ISH
"I'm going to drain the pool today Mr. Gatsby."

MICKEY
Dickey.

JOHN
Should we wait?

NAN
"Leaves'll be falling pretty soon--"

MICKEY
Jacket.

ISH
"Leaves'll be falling pretty soon--"

(silence on stage)

DAY
(walkie) I want you to know that I love you all and assume you have a plan. Surprise me.

MICKEY
Tie. John, follow my lead.

JOHN
What are we doing?

MICKEY
(taking JOHN onstage, making up something to fill the time) I lead.

NAN
"And then there's always the trouble with the pipes."

ISH
"And then there's always the trouble with the pipes."

NAN
I'm going to drain the pool today, Mr. Gatsby. Leaves'll be falling pretty soon, and then there's always trouble with the pipes.

ISH
I'm going to drain the pool today, Mr. Gatsby. Leaves'll be falling pretty soon, and then there's always the trouble with the pipes.

NAN
Go. You've got this.

(ISH enters onstage. PETER saunters in, entertained)

PETER
The kid wet himself. They changed his pants and then he pooped himself.

NAN
We just sent the noob onstage for his theatrical debut.

PETER
What? *(Seeing ISH)* Oh shit!

(NAN and PETER's scene starts after ISH's line)

ISH *(as BUTLER)*
I'm going to drain the pool today, Mr. Gatsby.

(pause) The leaves are going to fall. *(pause)* It's autumn. And they'll... get stuck?

GATSBY
Don't do it today. You know, old sport, I've never used that pool, all summer?

NICK
Twelve minutes to my train. I'll call you up.

GATSBY
Do, old sport.

NICK
I'll call you about noon.

GATSBY
I suppose Daisy'll call, too.

NICK
I suppose so.

GATSBY
Well, good-by.

NICK
They're a rotten crowd! You're worth the whole damn bunch put together!

PETER and NAN
Yes!

(They high five)

PETER
(overlapping Gatsby's line "Don't do it today.") No! Did you see that? He saluted! That's so awesome.

NAN
Isn't he supposed to exit?

PETER
Hey! Hey! Psst!

NAN
Exit! Exit!

PETER
Dude! Hey, dude! Hey! Get over here!

(ISH exits stage, still saluting)

PETER
You are getting so many beers bought for you!

(ELIZABETH re-enters)

NAN
Give me a hug, you little sh--!

(ISH vomits all over her)

NAN
This was a period dress.

ISH
I'm sorry, I'm so sorry. I'm really sorry. *(etc.)*

NICK
He must have looked up at an unfamiliar sky through frightening leaves and shivered as he found what a grotesque thing a rose is and how raw the sunlight was upon the scarcely created grass. A new world, material without being real, where poor ghosts, breathing dreams like air, drifted fortuitously about... like that ashen, fantastic figure gliding towards him through the amorphous trees.

ELIZABETH
(overlapping NICK's line) Yay! We're Barf Buddies!

(two gunshots)

PETER
Do you want a towel?

NICK
Gatsby believed in the green light, the orgiastic future that year by year recedes from us. It eluded us then, but that's no matter - tomorrow we will run faster, stretch out our arms farther. ... and one fine morning --- So we beat on, boats against the current, borne back ceaselessly into the past.

(Silence. Pause. A trickle of applause turns into a torrent)

PETER
Let's go! Curtain call!

(NAN and PETER enter on stage)

ISH
Should I go out there?

ELIZABETH
It's too late now. What, you need people to clap for you? *(She slow claps for him)*

Scene 6 - Opening Night Party

ISH
On to the opening night party... Duties done, the cast, surrounded by friends and strangers alike, finally celebrate-- Lights and sound - go.

(KAKU enters - a blast of dance music and theatrical lighting. KAKU is somehow instantly part of the party - are there two of him?)

KAKU
You want some shrooms?

ISH
I'm good.

KAKU
Can you hold on to this bag, then? Otherwise I have a tendency to get high and take all of it at once!

ISH
It's like flying to a Caribbean island in the middle of winter and it's suddenly summer!

KAKU
What are you talking about?

ISH
Opening night parties!

KAKU
Stop being in a play and start having fun.

(music, dancing, drugs. The music slows. Impressionism expands)

ASHLEY
Everybody stop!

(pause)

ASHLEY
Review's up!

(Everyone gets on a device and begins to read...)

Review 1 - The Green Light

ARTHUR
"A Great Gatsby --" by Arthur Williamson, theatre critic for The Times

It would be easy to dismiss Elizabeth Fricke's new stage adaptation of F. Scott Fitzgerald's 1925 compulsory classic as another entry into that tired theatrical subgenre - Absurdist Political-provocation Piece. These didactic romps are conceived to shake up a mostly white, mostly wealthy audience's notions of race and/or gender by presenting a presumably never-before-attempted grad-school level reimagining of something so familiar, so vanilla, that you (wealthy, white, comfortable) will be startled spitless out of your seat. It would be easy to dismiss this Great Gatsby for that reason because it is all of those things. But, like a good cocktail poured by a true mixologist, it is also more than the sum of those intoxicants.

You see, most directors would truly be content to cast some pretty young things as the West Egg elites, inject the stage with Roaring Twenty's jazz and brightly colored linen and then smash it with the dusty hommes des terres of the Wilsons. But Miss Fricke has axes to grind and this stalwart oak (or is it teak) of American Literature has a rather large target on it's trunk. Not content to simply blow the sulphur of Anti-Semitism and racism into the fresh breeze of Fitzgerald's prose (it's already in there, give a man enough rope to hang himself...) Fricke explodes upon the stage an army of calculated stereotypes all mashing up against each other like a great party or a bloody war.

If all of this sounds an improbable, insulting, dizzying affair: it is. But it is also thoughtful, well-acted, and frankly, a lot of fun. It's hard to get this style right. But, as if the Traditional Casting Gods were paper tigers to be thoroughly blown away, Fricke has had the inspiration to cast Ugandan actor Mickey Ndwaddeewazibwa as the titular Jay Gatsby. Mr. N. navigates this audacious and confounding menagerie with the ease and confidence the rest of the world expects from an American capitalist hero. This savvy African-Englishman never let's his Harlem drawl drop - when he let's fly Gatsby's trademark "Old Sport", the whole room seemed to lean in to him and grin with recognition.

Of course, there is something rotten in the state of West Egg, and once the shell starts to crack, the truth starts to flow out. Fitzgerald is famous for saying that there are no second acts in American lives, but it's in the second act that this production really comes to life. You settle into the garish conceits: and the Gordian Knot of racial, religious and socio-economic commentary twists in your hand, tempting you to cut it, while you simultaneously marvel at and blame yourself for how it got so complicated.

3 ½ stars.

Coda 1 - The Green Light

ELIZABETH
Yes! We did it! Gatsby!

BEN
Congratulations!

(BEN is standing in the door holding a bottle of champagne)

BEN
To a great Gatsby! To the green light! And to the white whale it heralds!

(Cheers)

END OF ACT ONE

ACT II

Ish 3 - The Horror of Judgement

(It is morning, after the party. ISH enters with a large bag and a huge poster copy of Arthur's review over his head)

ISH
Act Two, go. You may have some sense now of what this review - and Arthur Williamson's good opinion in general - meant to Bad Settlement.

NAN
We're sold out next week and the week after that, but we have 8 tickets for the matinee next Sunday.

ISH
At the time, I too was swept up in the excitement that seats may be filled to overflowing. That our little show was a river about to meet the sea.

(PETER and DAY enter, crossing, from opposite sides. Wordlessly, they execute a flawless moving "high five" or "up top". They exit)

ISH
But behind the mask of relief and excitement at our windfall, there was something else lurking behind it: a dim horror of the uncontrollable randomness of human opinion.

NAN
(at the theatre) For the last six available tickets on a Saturday night? I do think fifty dollars is a fair price. Someone will pay it. It's called Dynamic Pricing because it's fucking exciting.

ISH
We all face judgment - from perfect strangers, from our employers, from our gods, from ourselves. Yearly, weekly, daily, it comes for us: Judgment, that pregnant opinion we pack with the possibility that it may be truth... that it will sum up our entire existence in one horrible simplicity. And nowhere outside of a courtroom does it reach a more feverish pitch than in the conversation between Artist and Critic.

JOHN
Which pull quote do you like better: "Like a great party or a bloody war" or "thoughtful, well-acted and frankly a lot of fun"? *(ISH shrugs)* Thanks, man.

ISH
One of the things I love about the theatre is that it exists only here, only now. Apologies to all the professors of literature out there but theatre is not on the page. It's not on a screen. After the final performance, besides the landfill and drunken tales, the only place a production swims on in the vast ocean of human endeavor is in its reviews.

(ELIZABETH approaches the poster ISH is holding with JOAO in tow)

ELIZABETH
I'm telling you: it can be bigger. And that is what she said.

ISH
They are shadows of each other: performance and criticism. Performance without criticism is art in a vacuum. Criticism without performance is simply being grumpy. They love each other, they hate each other, but most of all: they need each other. Work grows by excellence in criticism and criticism grows by excellence in work.

NAN
(on the phone) We're holding a gala closing night. Because we can afford to. It's what you do when you have sold out show - you spend that money to make even more money.

ISH
I know many artists who refuse to read their reviews. There's an idealism in this that I admire. But can you imagine the opposite? A critic that ignores performance? I don't even know what that is... Journalism? Context? Academia? I shudder to think of it's power.

NAN
(to MICKEY, who is crossing through) Congratulations on the review!

MICKEY
What review?

NAN
(exiting after MICKEY) Do you want me to read

it to you verbatim?

ISH

I prefer the other path - read everything. If art is a conversation, then criticism is a conversation. The more opinions I seek, the more chances someone will give me a useful note. In a hundred opinions, maybe one has the ability to move me.

This is my way of countering the horror that lurks beneath judgment - look it in the eye and keep asking it more questions. And always try to remember that opinion is not fact and that honesty is not truth. Especially my own.

But this too is an ideal. Some people's opinions we simply value more than others. And some people know that and use it to their advantage. Nothing can kill a sailor like a terrified whale, but nothing can kill a soul like a calculated judgement.

Scene 7 - Arrival

(The front door of the theatre opens. A young man enters with a few large suitcases)

AMOS
Wow. Some things never change. Crazy!

ISH
Hey!

AMOS
Hey. Home. You know, I saw my very first play here. I was ten. My parents took me to see The Count of Monte Cristo. Dennis whats-his-name played Edmund Dantes and when Fernand committed suicide, when I realized what a badass The Count was, I was done for.

ISH
Can I help you?

AMOS
Yeah, thanks man. *(He sets his bags down in front of ISH)* Where am I staying?

ISH
You're Amos! Amos Delaney! So nice to meet

you! Everyone's going to be thrilled you're here. How was your flight?

AMOS
So good. I washed some Percoset down with a glass of wine while we waited for coach to board. Now me crashy.

ISH
Let me find Day...

AMOS
Awwww. I want a drink. Is the bar open?

ISH
I could go ask Nan...

AMOS
No worries, bro. Aw. Day's still here? She's the best. I'm so thirsty.

ISH
Well, why don't you wait in the lounge and I'll have Day or Nan come meet you.

AMOS
Sweet! Thanks, boss. Can you grab my bags?

ISH
Oh, I have to deliver this first.

AMOS
No worries. Just make sure my bags get to the crash pad. What's in the bag?

ISH
We had opening night of Gatsby last night and *(he takes Beary Grant out of the bag)* Beary Grant made a guest appearance.

(pause)

AMOS
Get that the fuck away from me.

ISH
What?

AMOS
Get it the fuck away from me I'm fucking serious. I will freak out.

(ISH puts it back in the bag. NAN enters)

NAN
Amos Delaney as I live and breathe.

AMOS
Nan Tucci. You looks good. *(He spins her into him and dips her)*

NAN
Okay. Okay. Did you just get in? You know we have Balm rehearsal tonight, right?

AMOS
What day is it?

NAN
Monday.

AMOS
Cool. So stoked. Do you have a script?

(They exit)

ISH
I'll just... get the bags...

DAY
(crossing) Production meeting!

ISH
Amos's bags-

DAY
Now. The Nesting Phase is over.

ISH
Yup.

Scene 8 - The Cabin Table

(The Board Room - the team has already gathered)

DAY
The Nesting Phase is over. Yay. But let's not get ahead of ourselves, because we seem to have skipped the Focus Phase... And moved straight into a Gathering Phase. Which means I have no idea if Ben will be here or not. *(The team is not pleased)* So. Welcome to the second production meeting for Moby Dick! I am excited to see everyone's research. For those of you new to this room, this is, in fact, my favorite part of production. Who wants to start?

JOHN
I do. Uh. So. I have this aural document. Instead of explaining it - I think I've talked to you all about it - I'd like to just fire it up and let it be the soundscape for the meeting.

(He starts the recording, it plays under the scene until denoted)

DAY
Great. Who's next?

JOHN
Oh - don't tell Ben that I actually deconstructed the sound effects from the first Moby Dick. That's the sound of Ahab's pipe hitting the water slowed down four-hundred percent. Just saying. There it is again. Go on.

DAY
Noted.

SYDNEY
Oh, I'll go, you bunch of white-livered harlots. *(uncovering his model)* Space! Transformation!

VAL
That is the most amazing model I've ever seen. Is that real water?

ASHLEY
Oh fuck you, Sydney.

(The table circles the model, taking pictures, passing around the photos, making a mess, flattering SYDNEY)

DAY
Nicely done, as usual Mr. Smythe.

ASHLEY
Nice. Nicely done. Credit where credit is due, my friend. I applaud you, sir. That's right, take a bow. *(SYDNEY does)* Gah! If only I had anticipated your overproduced apple-polishing... hit it, Liz!

(ELIZABETH turns the lights out)

ELIZABETH
Ah hahaha! E-lizabeth.

(Pop. ASHLEY has constructed an elaborate grid of flashlights that turns SYDNEY's model into a work of art)

ASHLEY
Lights up on a lighting presentation. Ben, you're really missing out on this one, buddy. *(ASHLEY performs a veritable light dance)*

ASHLEY
And... scene.

SYDNEY
Bravo.

DAY
Who's next? Val?

VAL
Uh. I'm kind of nervous. Especially without Ben here...

DAY
It's fine. Whatever you have...

VAL
So. Okay. *(she pulls out a duffel bag)* I knitted the story of Moby Dick... *(She pulls out the craziest, awesomest thing ever done with soft goods and the soundtrack runs out)* Or, I guess, the feeling of Moby Dick, texturally? And I worked in all these fabric samples while listening to the Aural Document that John gave us. Thanks, by the way, it's really really great.

JOHN
You're welcome...

VAL
So, I guess this is kind of the Fabric Document.

I'm not sure how to pass this around.

(silence)

DAY
Thanks, Val. All right. Peter, since Fights are new to the room, I don't expect you to have anything. So...

(BEN enters applauding. He has a fast food bag with him)

BEN
Good morning, Room of Sages. I am late and I own that. A lot has happened since the last time we met. We're all older. Crops were harvested. The great Great Gatsby. *(He starts a room full of applause)* And... this... *(he pulls out a copy of the script and lays it on the table)*

MICKEY
Huzzah!

BEN
Huzzah, indeed.

PETER
Is that it?

BEN
That's it. Three lean acts. You helped me finish it.

ELIZABETH
Who, little old me?

BEN
The thing about Moby Dick... he's a slippery fish. It took seeing Gatsby for me to See it... It was so fresh. So vital. It was exactly how we needed

the journey of the season to begin. And that got me thinking. Imagine that: Moby Dick getting me thinking!

(Oh, that guy!)

BEN
Moby Dick is an adventure novel. I want to lay that adventure like a transparency, like a gel over this wonderful minimalism we've pared it down to. Our Moby Dick is the memory of adventure. It's the Odyssey. It's Don Quixote. It's... the Wizard of Oz! That's it! We start in the monochromatia of New Bedford and Nantucket and as the ship casts off -- Technicolor!

For the first time, we see this blue of the water, the warmth of the deck, the exotic lines of the parti-colored crew. Val, I think you were right - we see that crisp newness of their bland garments transform into the exotic lines of every nation.

VAL
So, no more Greek?

BEN
No. No no -- still Greek. But think more like the Greek Islands. More adventure. It's the story we all have of how green the grass was, how strange and yet wise the new and curious people were, how the houses were shaped like toys -- the story of the first new place we loved outside our homes - the place our youthful heart yearns to reclaim. It's almost a spiritual notion... Hm. And it's in the round. 360 degrees. Like the world!

PETER
Uhhhhh.

JOAO
If we are in the round, we cannot retract the platform.

BEN
Of course. Because you were right all along, Joao -- the platform has to raise. Especially now that the platform can no longer be a square - *(He pulls out a drawing and shows it to SYDNEY)* This outline of a boat finally gives us the vertical line pushing forward - pushing towards adventure - until we culminate in the boat not sinking, but rising and our Ishmael discovered adrift in the true water and wreck of his life at the end.

JOAO
It's very ambitious.

BEN
The moment Balm closes I'd love to have the platform prepped for it's transformation. We'll need time to rehearse on it. And the rigging. I forgot. We need places for Ishmael to escape up - giant rope ladders that splay out over the audience. Imagine Ishmael hanging right above you, - physical proximity and danger palpable. That's adventure. Ashley, you've got your work cut out for you. I am late for a matinee of Wit - I hope the dear woman is still alive. If anyone has any questions, filter them through Elizabeth, our accomplished assistant director.

(As suddenly as he arrived. He's gone. Everyone looks at ELIZABETH)

JOAO
This boat... does not make me happy. Eighty-one hundred. And that is not counting the truss and rigging. Fifteen thousand, all told.

NAN
Gulp.

SYDNEY
Good to know.

ELIZABETH
No one freak out.

ASHLEY
What the Gel?

ELIZABETH
Day, when are final designs due?

DAY
One week.

ELIZABETH
Great. Let's all sleep on this and re-jigger the old brains and starting tomorrow, I'll make myself available for one-on-one's where we can hash this out for reals and set some new deadlines that won't crush anyone's soul. Fair?

DAY
Before we all go meditate - the next production meeting was scheduled for Monday. What do you say we bump it up a few days? I'll send out some calendars and we'll find a time. Meeting adjourned. Thank you all for being awesome.

(Everyone begins to pack up and leave)

PETER
(on his way out) Did Amos make it in?

NAN
You know he did, Peter.

PETER
No, I didn't know. Now I know. Amos is here. Good. Good!

NAN
Is it good?

ELIZABETH
(on her way past) It's good. It's so good it's good-tastic.

PETER
I said it was good, so it's good.

DAY
Don't look too happy

NAN
(giving DAY a parcel) Day, can you deliver this to Ben? It slipped my mind.

DAY
I can't imagine why. (reading it) Another one?

NAN
Maybe he's in lurve.

DAY
I'll deliver it.

Scene 9 - Does That Answer Your Question?

NAN
Do you know why I kill myself fundraising, casting, administrating and acting on top of all that? Because Ben Adonna is a great artist. And like every great artist, he needs help running a business. I don't know if I'd trust an artist that doesn't.

ELIZABETH
Ben is a hiring genius. He always gets the best people. I think he sees a little bit of himself in me… you know when he was young and crazy and did that first version of Moby Dick with Red Letter. It was a disaster. I wish I'd seen it!

JOHN
The first Moby Dick? The one he did with Red Letter? It was, gosh, twenty years ago? It was actually my first show. I played Ahab's son in a fantasy. I was eight. Arthur's review was… we don't like to mention it.

KAKU
Arthur panned that play. The worst review anyone

has ever read. It's legendary. It's not online and only a few copies remain. They say if you read the second paragraph, you go mad. MAD!

MICKEY
You know he was Tyrone Guthrie's assistant on the last play he ever directed: Uncle Vanya, 1969 at the Minneapolis Theatre. I've seen Ben drunk precisely once. Guthrie was all he would talk about.

KAKU
Tyrone Guthrie? A famous director, doll-face. Apparently everyone who worked for him adored the man. He "found" Olivier, Richardson, Laughton, I think. Famous actors, sweetie. They called him the "Audience of a Thousand".

JOAO
Ben? He is *(gesture)*. But sometimes he is... not.

ASHLEY
This is my thirty-fourth play with Ben. The first thirty-three were the hardest. But seriously: he's a genius. An ass-hole, but a genius. At some point it doesn't matter when you're working with quality.

SYDNEY
I've known the bugger for twenty years: he's never where he's supposed to be when he's supposed to be there. And I've never seen him sleep. I don't think he does. And I knew him when he drank.

PETER
Do you wanna know the weirdest thing about him? He runs hot. Not like meh-I've-got-a-

fever hot. Like hot hot. Like holy-shit-I-just-touched-the-oven-hot. Swear to God.

KAKU
You did what, now? Don't ever listen to Peter Trellis, he's a fraternity of one.

PETER
You know he's a synesthete? He sees sounds. Music, words. It's incredible. Ask him sometime what color A flat is.

KAKU
Oh no, that's true.

VAL
He doesn't scare me, but when he walks in the room I feel like I've done something wrong.

DAY
When you've known someone long enough, answering that question gets harder. You've seen different versions. You've seen them change. What's normal can be one thing, then what's normal is abnormality. You have to digest whoever comes through that door and make it normal to yourself. Otherwise: That Way Madness Lies. Does that answer your question?

ISH
Yes. I think so. Thanks, Day.

Balm in Gilead. Go.

Big 1 - A Very Attractive Looking Cast

(The Constellation Theatre. Everyone is there.)

PETER
Welcome everyone to rehearsal for Balm in Gilead! You are a very attractive looking cast! I mean that.

ISH
Peter, it turns out, started every rehearsal like that. The first day, it continued like this...

PETER
Day, are we all met?

DAY
We are!

PETER
Many of you may recognize me: I am Peter Trellis. I am your director. You may also recognize our set, because it's this set. You see, we don't have a budget. But that's okay. It's okay. It's so okay, it's like we planned it. You see, we're gonna get our hands dirty, like the tramps and junkies that we are. This is Sydney and this is

Val. How dirty are your hands, guys?

SYDNEY
Very, very dirty.

VAL
So dirty.

PETER
And why are your hands so dirty?

SYDNEY
Well, because we've stuck them in every dumpster and gnat-infested alley in the city.

PETER
Sydney, why would I ask you to do that? Gross.

SYDNEY
Because we have a plan.

PETER
Because. We have. A plan. We are going to dumpster dive for every prop, every set-dressing and every person-dressing in the show. I am so excited, I've got a chub--

(BEN has entered)

PETER
Hello, Ben.

BEN
Sorry to interrupt Peter, but now that everyone is here, I want to take a moment to welcome this crew, this entire crew, to Bad Settlement Theatre Company. *(the company cheers)* Looking around this room, I see the fruit of a very long tending that has finally ripened. You have been brought here, across time and space to translate - into

a living, breathing testament - the power of Love and Brotherhood and yes, fear and ignorance. This work means something to me. It stirs something in me. Let's give this to a world that so desperately needs it. We are the poor, crazy souls who have brought ourselves here to bring Awesome Power to bear on one impossible aim: Moby Dick. Let's open our books to the beginning.

DAY and PETER
Ben--

AMOS
I don't mean to be a dick, but I don't have the script yet.

BEN
You're not being A Dick. We won't need our scripts quite yet. You can use one of my books.

DAY
Ben--

BEN
Shall we? Let's read Chapter One, now that we're all here. Peter, is that okay with you?

PETER
Sure. Sure.

DAY
Are you sure, Peter?

PETER
Yeah. Yeah. Let's do this.

BEN
Bene. Amos, can you take the first line?

AMOS
Yeah. Okay. Etymology. *(pause)* Oh… Supplied by a late consumptive Usher-

BEN
Call me Ishmael.

AMOS
Hm?

BEN
Call me Ishmael.

MICKEY
Page twelve.

AMOS
Oh, shit, sorry. Xii twelve or 12 twelve?

BEN
12 Twelve.

ELIZABETH
It's right after 11 eleven.

AMOS
Call me Ishmael. One.

ELIZABETH
That's a note, you don't have to read those.

AMOS
Sweet. Call me Ishmael.

ELIZABETH
Some years ago - never mind how long precisely - having little or no money in my purse (ha) and nothing in particular to interest me on shore, I thought I would sail about a little and see the watery part of the world.

KAKU
It is a way I have of driving off the spleen, and regulating the circulation. *(pause)* Your turn.

ISH
Oh. Uh. Whenever I feel myself growing grim about the mouth; whenever it is a damp, drizzly November in my soul; whenever I find myself involuntarily pausing before coffin warehouses, and bringing up the rear of every funeral I meet; and especially whenever my hypos get such an upperhand of me, that it requires a strong moral principle to prevent me from deliberately stepping into the street, and methodically knocking people's hats off - then, I account it high time to get to sea as soon as I can.

DAY
This is my substitute for pistol and ball.

(The cast continues reading the first chapter under this, skipping to the end where suggested)

ISH
As the company passed around the words, handing them off like some precious egg to the person beside them, I had the most amazing feeling of reverence. Like many of you, I'm sure, I have tried to read this book a dozen times. Never once had I felt an iota of what passed between us for fourteen minutes and twelve seconds. What a talented actor can do with a word like--

NAN
Circumambulate (the city--)

ISH
-- is a kind of magic that makes you lean forward

in your seat. That is the addiction of live theatre, when words tumble out of your mouth and an audience leans into you for more. As the last words of the first chapter fell from the last mouth--

MICKEY
By reason of these things, then, the whaling voyage was welcome; the great flood-gates of the wonder-world swung open, and in the wild conceits that swayed me to my purpose, two and two there floated into my inmost soul, endless processions of the whale, and, midmost of them all, one grand hooded phantom, like a snow hill in the air.

BEN
That was lovely. If anyone needs me this evening, I'll be at the final preview of As Bees in Honey Drown at Warped Woof Theatre.

PETER
I hate that play. Can we have Balm rehearsal now?

DAY
We need to take ten. Ben, can I talk to you?

PETER
Great. That's ten, everyone.

(The light coalesces around BEN and DAY as the cast goes to their bags, gets water, snacks, looks at lines)

DAY
Ben--

BEN
Day, I'd love to carve out the first thirty minutes

of each rehearsal for reading the book. I know this seems extraordinary. I know you want to fight this with every fiber of your being. But you saw what just happened there. I know you did.

DAY
Thirty minutes, Ben--

BEN
Talk to Peter. He'll take it hard at first, but he knows it's the right thing to do. The rest will fall in line if we present a united front.

DAY
I'll talk to him.

BEN
Thank you.

BIG 2 - It's Like A Metaphor

(The cast is reading the end of Chapter 7 - The Chapel)

ISH
A few days later...

NAN
Yes, there is death in this business of whaling - a speechlessly quick chaotic bundling of a man into Eternity.

AMOS
But what then?

BEN
Methinks we have hugely mistaken this matter of Life and Death--

ELIZABETH
Methinks--

BEN
Methinks that what they call my shadow here on earth is my true substance.

ELIZABETH
Me--

BEN
Methinks that in looking at things spiritual, we are too much like oysters observing the sun through the water, and thinking that thick water the thinnest of air. Methinks my body is but the lees of my better being. In fact, take my body who will, take it I say, it is not me. Hm.

ELIZABETH
And therefore three cheers for Nantucket; and come a stove boat and stove body when they will, for stave my soul, Jove himself cannot.

BEN
Good read, everyone. I'll be at the final preview of Pal Joey tonight--

PETER
I hate that play...

BEN
-- so catch me before that with any questions. Peter, they're all yours.

PETER
Great. Day, are we all met?

DAY
We are not.

PETER
Who are we missing?

BEN
Amos has a Moby Dick fitting. Amos, why don't we talk a bit on the way?

AMOS
Sure thing, Captain. See you suckers in an hour.

(They leave)

PETER
We'll miss you buddy. Have a great Dick fitting. Because who wouldn't be itching at the chance to rehearse one of the best sex scenes in the American theatre cannon? It's like dirty, salty candy.

(SYDNEY and VAL enter with garbage bags)

SYDNEY
Peter--

PETER
Perfect timing. Plan B! Rooting through garbage in the lobby, everyone! It's like a metaphor!

SCENE 10 - HAVE A GRAPE

(As everyone sifts through the garbage, finding things for the show, the lights coalesce on SYDNEY and VAL)

SYDNEY
I've done some pretty terrible things in my life--

VAL
Ugh. Me. Too. I once worked for this outdoor show in Arkansas, in the summer. It was like a cross between Shakespeare-in-the-Park and a Church Play. But it was about these racist hillbillies, right? It was very popular. And the director wanted it really authentic. Like really authentic - so we weren't allowed to wash or fix any of the actors costumes. If they wanted their clothes cleaned or darned, the women in the show had to do it during a performance. There were forty people in the play. And horses. And sheep. And a chicken. So my job for three months was to gather up all these sweaty, bloody, snotty things - and we weren't allowed to hang

them up either. We just dropped them in piles. There were flies, spiders... one of the guys got mold in his shoes. Ugh. The best stories cost you something though, I guess. It's nice to be able to get to know each other. Trade war stories about theatre...

SYDNEY
I wasn't talking about theatre. I've just done rotten, dirty, disgusting things. In life. Emotionally, physically. Spiritually. I'm not complaining, mind you - I got paid for some of it. But this - this is the new bottom. And I'm really, really proud of that.

VAL
Oh?

SYDNEY
I am. Wondering if the next bag will hold a mostly-used roll of duct tape or some mostly coherent undergarments has helped me reassess the meaning of hope. I think our job, as artists, is to continuously reassess all meaning by continuously discovering lower and lower origins of human baseness. And then share it with each other. We're like the Lewis's and Clark's of shit.

VAL
Mm. Mm-hm.

SYDNEY
For instance - have a grape.

VAL
Nn-nn.

SYDNEY
Then watch me eat it. *(pause)* Have it your way.

Sometimes imagination is stronger, anyway. Mmmmm.

VAL
If you find anything with a zipper, cut it off for me.

SYDNEY
Will do.

ISH
A couple days and several garbage bags later, I learned that success in film doesn't necessarily translate into success on stage.

BIG 3 - A REALLY SCARY BEAN GUY

(PETER, DAY and ISH are watching rehearsals. Ben is not there)

JOE
Look, you want to know something? You want to know something? I knew what I was doing. I keep a sharp lookout for myself, you don't have to worry about that. I watch people and size them up. And this guy Chuckles you heard me mention?

DARLENE
Yeah?

JOE
The guy who had someone call me back at the cafe? Now, this guy is probably the most important pusher - he doesn't push himself, but he supplies - and you don't screw around with him. I got in touch with Chuckles a while back and told him I wanted to get cut in. Make some dough around the neighborhood. Hell, he'd been watching me for weeks. Months! And we made this deal--

PETER
Hold! Nan, great job. Good listening. Amos... Chuckles, man. Do you like the guy?

AMOS
I mean, they have to call him Chuckles for some reason. In my backstory that I wrote, he was a clown for childrens' birthday parties and then started dealing to parents.

PETER
Okay. Okay. But now, he's the scariest dude on upper Broadway. Children run into their houses when they see him coming. Have you ever seen The Wire?

AMOS
No, but I worked with a guy who was in it. Stand-up guy.

PETER
Imagine the Boogie Man. Whatever the Boogie Man was for you when you were a kid.

AMOS
K. Got it.

PETER
You just made a deal with the Boogie Man to sell nightmares. But you've got it. You're on top of it. You know if you make one wrong move, he's gonna slice you, but you're... you got it. And that line about him not pushing any more. Day, what is it?

DAY
Uh... "Now this guy is probably the most important pusher - he doesn't push himself, but he

supplies - and you don't screw around with him."

PETER
You know what he's saying about "he doesn't push himself"?

AMOS
Yeah, yeah totally.

PETER
Can you paraphrase it for me?

AMOS
So this Chuckles clown, he kinda sits around and doesn't do anything ambitious and has other people do the work for him.

PETER
Okay. Okay. Or... try it that Chuckles is super ambitious and so smart that he doesn't "deal drugs" or "Push" himself but makes all the fat cash by giving people drugs to sell.

AMOS
Isn't he still selling drugs then, technically.

NAN
I guess technically he is.

PETER
I... yeah. Thanks, Nan. But it's more like he's selling to the sellers. Right? He's not the coffee shop, he's the guy selling the coffee shop the beans.

AMOS
He's the bean monster.

PETER
A really scary bean guy.

AMOS
Yeah.

PETER
Great, from the top!

DAY
We need a ten.

PETER
Even better! Let's take a ten!

DAY
(to ISH) Can I see you for a second?

ELIZABETH
Oh no! Is he fired? You're so fired.

DAY
You're not fired. I need you to take this package to Ben's room. Leave it on the little table.

ISH
Where?

DAY
It's the only table. Here's the key.

ISH
Uh.

DAY
It won't bite. Don't worry, he's at the final preview for Man and Superman.

PETER
I love that play.

DAY
Go. You've got five minutes. Room 135.

SCENE 11 - ROOM 135

ISH
And so... down the hall I went to Room 135 with a package, stamped and re-stamped so that its contents from Fay Awee, Lotus Publishing, Acre, Israel, could reach their final destination at my hands.

(ISH knocks in the door)

ISH
Hello? *(He let's himself in)*

(The furniture has been removed, and a single, naked bulb hangs from the ceiling. One wall is plastered with pages from a book, hundreds of them - meticulously highlighted and interconnected with a web of red strings and pins that would confound a homicide detective)

ISH
(reading) "Chapter One: Loomings.

BEN's VOICE
"Call me Ishmael." *(ISH follows a red string from Ishmael)* "Chapter 7: The Chapel. Yes, Ishmael,

the same fate may be thine." *(He follow another sting)* "I, Ishmael, was one of that crew; my shouts had gone up with the rest; my oath had been welded with theirs."

(In the middle of the wall is another project - newspaper clippings in the shape of a man)

ARTHUR'S VOICE
(reading) "Interwoven Theatre's "Wit" Needs Sharpening". "The Honey Pours Slowly as These "Bees" Drown". "A Fine "Pal" in this "Joey"". "A Great Gatsby:--

Image of ARTHUR
--by Arthur Williamson".

(Arthur's face breaks through the head of the newspaper figure. ISH drops the package and runs terrified from the room)

ISH
That's technically called Magical Realism. And this is technically called a Fundraiser. Lights and sound. Go.

Scene 12 - The Gam

(A song very obviously appealing to rich 55-64 year old white women plays. Perhaps "Downtown" or "To Sir With Love". The theatre is tastefully decorated. There are hors d'oeuvres and wine. A mic on a stand sits on the Gatsby stage. The music starts to fade as NAN steps to the mic. BEN stands behind her)

NAN
Good evening. Hi, everybody. I hate to interrupt the party. Our thanks to Radcliffe Distributions for the wine and snacks. They're very tasteful. For those of you who don't know me, I'm Nan Tucci, I'm the Associate Artistic Director of Bad Settlement Theatre Company. Welcome to closing night of our hit show, The Great Gatsby, directed by Elizabeth Fricke.

(Applause)

NAN
Thank you, thank you. As many of you may know, Bad Settlement Theatre Company grew out of a desire to bring our community a different kind

of storytelling. And what I appreciate, and am humbled by, is how each of you continuing friends of the company has trusted us and stood by us the whole way. You trusted us with our shared vision of what a theatre company could be. So... what you've all "Ben" waiting for - the next great chapter in bringing you the very best in theatre experiences; Moby Dick, by our prestigious and very charming artistic director, Ben Adonna.

(Applause)

NAN
If you've never read Moby Dick - don't worry, I won't spoil anything (They all die!). But if you have, you know this book is a huge undertaking. We need your generosity to make our production the resounding success we know it can be. In fact... I'll hand this over to the man at the helm of the Pequod - Ben Adonna.

BEN
I am not at the helm of the Pequod. I am merely the shipwright, toiling in the drydock with a bucket of pitch in my hands, waiting for another shipment of strong, solid, American Oak to arrive. In Moby Dick, the Pequod isn't owned by Captain Ahab - it is owned by the citizens of Nantucket - shareholders who all have a stake. *(pause)* We need to get to the Season on the Line. That's where Moby Dick lies in wait - that's where our glorious future - Our Future - lies waiting for us to simply meet it there. But we need supplies to get there - clothes for the crew, harpoons for the kill, canvas for the sails, hemp for the lines, rigging, paint, wood. And this all

costs money.

(NAN tries to interrupt him)

BEN
Almost two hundred years ago, the people of Massachusetts, poor Puritan pacifists, got it into their heads that they could do something better than anyone else in the world. They looked at their neighbors and said: you, Folgers; you, Gardners; you, Coffins; you Starbucks, Shaws and Husseys - you are our gift to the world. Take these, our meager wages and show them what Americans can do! Show them how your Minds and your Hands and your Souls are meet to the task. And they did. With the support of their neighbors they went out and did what no American had ever done - they conquered the world. Not with armies, not with subterfuge, not with riches. But with talent. And all the rest, this American Dream, came from that.

(No one responds. BEN surrenders the mic to NAN)

NAN
There you have it: Moby Dick. DJ, turn it up! *(to BEN)* That was interesting.

BEN
Introduce me to someone important.

NAN
Why don't you let me handle it?

BEN
Who is the most important person in the room?

NAN
The richest, or the most influential?

BEN
The richest only if they can give six figures, the most influential only if they know Arthur or his editor.

NAN
Dorothy Whitehead just gave Stage Quest Theatre two hundred thousand for capital improvements, and Thomas Fourdelay is on the board of The Times. But I don't know him. He's a guest of the Grandersons.

BEN
Thomas, so nice of you to come…

(He exits to schmooze Thomas. Nan follows, smiling)

ISH
On the Closing Night Party!

PETER
Raise your glasses, ass holes!

ELIZABETH
Put 'em up!

PETER
Tonight, we put to rest one of our own: The Great Gatsby. That three-and-a-half-star fucker.

ELIZABETH
He lived a full life, a happy life. Ashes to asses, dust to dumpster.

MICKEY
The green light is dead! Long live the green light!

PETER
That's right! One last party in West Egg--

ELIZABETH
WOLFSHEIM!

PETER
--because tomorrow, it's back to Balm. In. ----

BIG 4 - A Knife in Gilead

(PETER, DAY, ISH *watching from their chairs*)

MICKEY *(as the STRANGER)*
(holding a very large syringe) Chuckles wanted you to know what hit you. Understand? That's a four-inch reach. You don't screw with Chuckles. Understand?

AMOS *(as JOE)*
I got something to tell him.

NAN *(as DARLENE)*
What? What is it?

AMOS *(as JOE)*
No! Come on.

(*The STRANGER/MICKEY stabs JOE/AMOS in the heart*)

PETER
Amos. Come here. Come here!

AMOS
Hey boss.

PETER
Hey. John, can I see Fick's knife?

JOHN
I don't know, Peter—

PETER
Just give me the knife.

(JOHN does)

PETER
You ever been in a knife fight, Amos?

AMOS
Yeah.

PETER
Really?!

AMOS
Yeah, I saw a dude pull a knife on this other dude in a club in Amsterdam.

PETER
Okay. Okay. Did he hold the knife like this? Right out in front, blade pointed up?

AMOS
Kinda like that, except it was one of those flicky knifes.

PETER
Oh it was the flicky kind. A... a switchblade? Was it, by chance, 1952 and these two greasers were in the sock-hop?

AMOS
Man, you are tweaking.

(During the following speech, BEN enters, and

PETER notices him)

PETER
Here's what I think, I think you have no idea what it's like to have your life actually threatened. For someone to actually get in your face and for you to know, for you to know that in one second, if you make the wrong choice, you're toast. I think the only thing you know about danger is that's what your stunt double is for.

NAN and DAY
Peter...

PETER
Hold on. Hold on. HI Ben. What's more Amos, I think you could handle it. That moment when someone finally snaps and tests you to see if you have the cajones. Because, I think Amos is smart enough to know when he's beaten and he'll walk away. But guess what, Joe isn't. In this play you'll have to imagine... or "act"... that this guy, this "Joe"... when he's faced with the Angel of Death... You see this knife. When you're in a real knife fight, not in the bleacher seats for an Amsterdam Fairy Dance, when you're in a real knife fight, you don't even know the other guy is holding it. And when he gets just close enough, BAM. And you're gone. Page 59, Joe and Darlene sit in a booth. You're doing great, Nan, keep it up.

DAY
We have to take a ten.

PETER
Perfect. Day, can I have a cigarette?

DAY
That's ten. *(giving PETER the cigarette she had behind her ear)* Smoke 'em if you got 'em.

AMOS
Thank you, ten.

PETER
(to BEN on his way out) Just softening him up for you, Ben. He's all yours in a couple of weeks.

Scene 13 - Boats Plural

(DAY intercepts BEN on his way out the door)

DAY
Ben?

JOHN
Puff puff?

DAY
I'll be out there in a minute. Ben, we need to talk.

BEN
If it's about Amos--

DAY
It's not. It's about the seven thousand dollars that left the set budget yesterday...

BEN
Oh, the boats.

DAY
Boats, plural?

BEN
It's fine. My friend in Japan will be building five

whaling boats for us and shipping them to us for first rehearsal. He's the only man for the job.

DAY
Joao?

BEN
Joao builds excellent, seaworthy boats. Paru builds exemplary stageworthy art.

DAY
We can't afford this--

BEN
The fundraiser closing night of Gatsby was very successful. The Grandersons will be sending us a check to cover the boats. Until then, we have to rob Peter to pay Paru. All right?

DAY
I don't like it.

BEN
Noted.

DAY
Ben, if we gave Joao detailed drawings, I'm sure--

BEN
It all works out in the end. I promise. Just say "Yes".

Scene 14 - an Excerpt

ISH
An excerpt from "Off the Grid - the Plots and Specials of a Terminally Mid-level Lighting Designer" by Ashley Salt. Self-published. Chapter 21 - "Just Say Yes". Lights… Go.

ASHLEY
When things got rough during tech, I would go back to my apartment, pour a glass of whiskey, and call my college lighting professor - my mentor, god rest her soul - to kvetch. There would be a little pause on the other end of the line after I finished an Olympian string of cuss words while she took a drag off her third unfiltered Lucky Strike and she'd say -- "But you said yes, right". "Yes, Molly," I'd say. "Well," another drag, "that's all you can do."

When I was out of instruments and the leko in channel 131 just couldn't run the barrel out any more, and the overhire electrician would ask if that was okay, I'd just say "Yes". It was all I could do and it made me feel like a hero.

When that charming professional juggler I'd been "not dating" for eight months asked me to marry him, and I thought, "isn't he gay" and then looked at my birth year, and just said "Yes"... it made me feel like an adult.

Now that I've been out of the game for a few years and have impressionable students of my own, I can look back and unequivocally say that those feelings and that advice is worth a bull's patooty.

It can be fun to suffer for a while, when the people are fun, the work is exciting and the pay helps you scrape by, but that first time I just said "No" to Herr Director and took a teaching job and bought a house - I didn't feel like a sell out or a quitter - I felt like I'd found my other half.

Saying "No" once in a while isn't a sin, it's a survival instinct. It isn't the enemy to art, it's the freedom to be yourself. And sometimes?... saying "No" is just fuckin' fun.

SCENE 15 - SHOULDERS

(DAY is in the booth, calling the show. Under the entire next scene, Balm in Gilead very quietly filters inside, starting with THE STRANGER's act two entrance)

ISH
There is no award for best dresser, no public accolades for curtain puller or actor cuer, set changer, laundry doer, audience usher. Nor is there an award for the most important person in the theatre night after night - the arbiter between actors, audience and crew, the leading actor in a dialog you never hear, performed in absentia through headsets and cue lights, and, heaven forfend, over god mics. I of course refer to that God of Fate - the Stage Manager.

DAY
Standby lights 356, sound 121. *(pause)* Lights... go. Sound... go. Standby backstage. Do we have the children ready?

ISH
(on com) Children standing.

DAY
Thank you children standing.

(BEN enters the booth, quietly. Pause)

BEN
Day, I just heard from Japan--

DAY
Ben, I'm calling a show.

BEN
The order was cancelled?

DAY
Joao took at look at the plans and said he could build all five boats for three thousand--

BEN
You cancelled my order? Day, I need those boats in less than a week.

DAY
We don't have that money in the budget, Ben.

BEN
You don't know that. Only I know that.

DAY
Standby, lights 358. We like Joao. We trust Joao.

BEN
Paru is the foremost Bunraku puppet-maker in the world.

DAY
Joao makes puppets--

BEN
Not these puppets! I'm not asking you to understand, I'm asking you to do your job. *(pause)* Your

job is to make the impossible possible.

DAY
Lights, go.

BEN
What aren't you telling me?

DAY
Standby sound 125. Standby children.

BEN
You're holding something back. Say what you want to say.

DAY
I am calling a show. I will be happy to join you in an hour and discuss whatever strikes your fancy, but until then, I can't say what I want to say, I have to say what I have to say. So... sound... go.

BEN
Fancy?

DAY
Children... Go. Standby lights 360, Sound 128.

BEN
This company doesn't exist to run Balm in Gilead. It exists because I say it exists. We could unplug all of this paraphernalia right this moment and not lose a breath of wind in our sails.

DAY
Then why don't you?

BEN
Balm in Gilead isn't our Moby Dick. Moby Dick

is our Moby Dick.

DAY
Lights. Go.

BEN
Without watching this rudderless Pequod, our audience can't achieve apotheosis.

DAY
Sound, go. Standby lights 365, Sound 130.

BEN
Say it.

DAY
Say what?

BEN
Whatever it is you're holding up in that refrigerated temper of yours.

DAY
Lights, go, sound... go. Standby lights 370, sound 135.

BEN
Your shoulders are creeping up...

DAY
Get out. That's what I'm holding on to, Ben. Get out and let me work.

BEN
Shoulders. You're holding back.

DAY
Lights and sound... go.

BEN
How is it, Balm in Gilead?

DAY
I can't tell.

BEN
Don't tell me you have no opinion.

DAY
I have lots of opinions.

BEN
And each one of them correctly apportioned into appropriate containers and stacked ever so neatly in the icebox of your mind. I need you let them out, one way or another. What do you think of Amos?

DAY
Stand by sound 136, lights 375. You could stand in the back and watch the show and form your own opinions.

BEN
I prefer it here. Ah, there's Arthur, his head cocked to one side, showing criticism. As if we didn't already know what he's here for! From here you can almost imagine it's all a pantomime: that no one's actually saying anything, but that the audience is hanging on every gesture. Storing up more and more tension until we release it and they have to spring from their seats and applaud simply because they can't help it.

DAY
We are not an audience hanging on your every gesture waiting for you to finish siphoning tension into us so that we can applaud you. Lights and sound go. Standby lights 380, sound 138, end of play.

BEN
I don't want your praise. I want your trust.

DAY
You want me to tell you how great you are.

BEN
No, I want people to talk about how great this company is.

(Pause)

BEN
Shoulders.

DAY
Lights and sound... go. Thank you, everyone. Tell the actors to get out of costume. Opening night party in the lobby. Excellent show.

(DAY takes her headphones off and leans back in her chair)

DAY
There is no check from the Grandersons.

(Applause)

BEN
Bravo! *(exiting)* Bravo! Bravo!

(Day sits, quietly watching through the booth)

ISH
To those of you who may be in a position of power - find a way to honor the humble stage manager. Because even if some deign to keep them unremembered, unnamed and forgotten - keep in mind, they remember you.

Scene 16 - Opening Night Party 2

ISH
On to the opening night party!

(KAKU enters - a blast of dance music and theatrical lighting. KAKU is somehow instantly part of the party - are there two of him? KAKU gives ISH a baggie of illicit substances. Music. Dancing. Drugs)

PETER
Everybody stop!

(Pause)

PETER
Review's up!

(Everyone gets on a device and begins to read...)

Review 2 - A Balm in Gilead

ARTHUR
"A "Balm" for the Ears…With One Exception"… by Arthur Williamson, theatre critic for The Times.

Expectation is the sharpest double-edged sword in live entertainment's arsenal. On the one hand, I cringe to imagine an audience showing up for A Balm in Gilead expecting a polite, melodic rhapsody (the title does sound practically pastoral). That kind of expectation is well to be subverted. The other edge, unfortunately, cuts at yours truly. You see, I had the incredible fortune of seeing the 1981 Steppenwolf production of Balm in Gilead, and it was the best night of theatre I've ever had. Talk about expectations…

This play attracts the best and most ambitious of acting ensembles because only the most copacetic of collaborators can even begin to parse it. Not only do you need an orchestra of virtuosi to pull it off, you need a world-class conductor to keep them all together. Thankfully, Bad Settlement has the kinetically-minded Peter Trellis to keep the pace. Mining his score for every ounce of violence, Trellis puts these actors through their paces on what can only be described as a counter-intuitive set. Pun intended. The diner's booths and tables (and a well-used bed in a nearby hotel) are suggested throughout by the actors lugging in various bits of street-side flotsam and jetsam and constructing their spaces themselves. In doing so, Trellis gives his junkies and hoods a measure of agency in their predicaments which leads to a kind of pulsing pity by the end of the night.

His actors (for the most part) never miss a note and have just the right kind of ear for each other's troubles and turbulence. Special attention should be paid to soloists Nan Tucci as new girl Darlene and Elizabeth Fricke who looks like she's having way too much fun as seen-it-all Ann. But when one instrument is out of tune, the whole orchestra can sound like a band. Grossly miscast and in need of a life-preserver among the terrific waves of this stormy sea, Amos Delaney treads water like a man cast adrift with no ship in sight. It's no fun to watch an actor drown, especially one with as much talent as Delaney, but it takes more than a shiny trumpet to make great music, there needs to be someone on the other end with breath and brains to make it sing. Delaney's Joe is supposed to be a soloist, but it's his accompaniment that shines. It's a testament to the composer, conductor and journeymen that this production stays afloat. Hopefully, someone will remember to turn the ship around and come back for the man overboard, and then this crew will really be something."

Two-and-a-half stars.

Coda 2 - Cistern & Buckets

(BEN interrupts. He holds a bottle of champagne)

BEN
A celebration is in order. We set out, not weeks ago, not months ago, but years ago to find ourselves here. Right here, right now. In this room. In this company.

Moby Dick is rising. We must prepare the way. There must be sacrifices. That is why Balm in Gilead will be closing two weeks early.

This is not a reflexion on anyone's work - this is a focusing on the work that is to come. Enjoy the rest of your run. You deserve it so much.

End Act Two

ACT III

MOBY DICK 1 - THE INTIMATE SELF

(The cast and crew have gathered for first rehearsal of Moby Dick. Enter BEN and FAYE)

ISH
Moby Dick. Chapter 1 - First Rehearsal. Go.

BEN
Welcome, everyone. Welcome. Here we are.

All dramatic adaptations of Moby Dick are doomed to inadequacy. They all fall short - because they must. The book is wicked. And dirty. Sly. Violent. Subtle. A dramatic encyclopedia. It seems to be both spiraling out of control and reacting to the smallest tug at the reigns of its author. It trots the globe while staying in one locale. It questions the very foundations of religion and then rescues us in the end from floating feet first into hell. It inspires interest and boredom, love and loathing.

All my life, I've watched other people fling answers at that whale. And some have stuck. But when he breaks free, and he always does, all that's left is a bent and twisted memory of an unsuccessful assault.

But we have things none of these other adapters had, even our past selves – this Room of Sages and an understanding of the spirit of the text that surpasses any since Melville himself.

I'd like you all to meet Faye Awee. Faye?

FAYE
(pulling her hood aside) Hello. I feel like I know all of you already. You have been very inspirational to me and I only hope I can impart to you a dram of what you have granted me. You have a great advocate in this man and he has revealed yourselves to me and you have changed me. You see…

The intimate self is infinitely porous. The most sensuous human moments are not about opening ourselves – that is exhibitionism – intimacy is when the world calls out to us to let it in and we give ourselves to one another. Intimacy is standing around a vat of spermaceti oil with thirty other people, squeezing the crude together, squeezing random hands, turning the slick, evasive slime between us into something thick and substantial, useful and romantic.

It feels like an exorcism, sometimes, consumed by this book as we are. But this work is not an exorcism – it is a prayer to be let further in. Come a little further in with me…

I come here to impart upon you two things that you did not know. First - that Moby-Dick was revealed to Herman Melville by none other than God himself. And second, that this book is the first and most sacred text of the Baha'i Faith.

"By my mercy and by my beauty! All that I have revealed unto thee with the tongue of power, and have written for thee with the pen of might, hath been in accordance with thy capacity and understanding, not with my state and the melody of my voice."

BEN
Ishmael survives because he is the prophet - he has seen. The production pivots on this. Our lives pivot on this.

Look around you. It is no mistake that you all have different talents, different beliefs. I'm not asking you to believe me -- I believe in you and in this book and in this story and I have belief enough for all of us.

Let the hunt begin!

(Applause. Cheering. Fear)

BEN
Amos, the first speech. This is it. Now is the moment. I need to see it.

AMOS
Now?

BEN
You can do this. Everyone, give Amos the space. Take your time.

(AMOS breathes, knows he needs to deliver)

AMOS
Call me... Ishmael.

BEN
Why are you pausing there? You have to treat Melville like Shakespeare - he gives you all the thoughts and all the pauses in the punctuation! They all know what you're going to say: don't make them wait. Again.

AMOS
Call me Ishmael. Some years ago - never mind how long precisely - having little or no money in my purse and nothing in particular to interest me on shore, I thought I would sail about a little and see the watery part of the world.

BEN
Stop. Like them.

AMOS
It is a way I have of driving off the spleen, and regulating the circulation.

BEN
Don't smile - like them. These are your best mates. And you have a secret. A three hour long secret.

AMOS
Whenever I feel myself growing grim about the mouth; whenever it is a damp, drizzly November in my soul; whenever I find myself involuntarily pausing before coffin warehouses--

BEN
Hold. Amos... this may be one of the most diffi-

cult roles in the theatrical canon. I've seen you play Hamlet. I've seen you grow from a spastic, overconfident boy into the man you are today. That is Ishmael. One more time.

AMOS
Call me Ishmael. Some years ago--

BEN
How many?

AMOS
--never mind how long precisely--

BEN
Like me. Like me!

AMOS
--having little or no money in my purse--

BEN
Hahaha!

AMOS
--and nothing, in particular, to interest me on land--

BEN
This time, fill the space. You are not just a soloist - you are The Soloist.

(An image of ARTHUR appears to AMOS, then disappears)

BEN
This time, make an entrance!

(AMOS exits. Pause)

BEN
And enter! *(pause)* Enter. *(pause)* Enter. *(pause)*

(DAY goes to the entrance)

DAY
He's gone.

BEN
Find him. Nan, can I talk to you?

(Everyone peels away to search the building)

Scene 17 - Trent

ISH
The search parties spread out. The Constellation isn't a large place, but it's large enough. I was the one who found him...

ISH
Amos? Amos?

AMOS
My name is Trent. *(pause)* Trent. It really is. Call me Trent. Trick or Trent. What's your name?

ISH
Your name is Amos.

AMOS
Does it have to be?

ISH
I think so.

AMOS
I don't. I made him up. He's a name. He's a thing. He's a profile. A hero. And Amos doesn't cry. Amos doesn't quit. Amos doesn't get talked to

like he's no one. He's Amos Delaney. He's Amos. I'm trash. I'm terrible. I'm the worst actor in the room. What if, what if I'm not Amos, and we only invite people who don't know Amos? But the reviewers, the reviewers know Amos. Then we don't invite them. We don't. We invite the other reviewers who don't know us. I know reviewers who don't know us. They know me. No. No. They know Amos. They know that Amos. What's your name? Can I call you Ishmael?

ISH
No.

AMOS
It's okay for you not to be Ishmael, but I have to be Trent?

ISH
You can be whoever you want, but I think here -- you have to be Amos.

AMOS
You be Amos.

ISH
I can't.

AMOS
You can. He's like a jacket.

ISH
I'm just me. The same person I always am.

AMOS
You're not. You're not, though. You're just like me. You're a jacket.

(NAN enters behind AMOS and goes to gather

him)

AMOS
I need to talk to Beary Grant.

(AMOS leaves, unceremoniously)

ISH
Whether or not Amos Delaney was real, he was invented to be invincible. In a profession where working from a place of absolute honesty is venerated, in all it's glory and gore, this man got a step closer to some inner honesty and it cost him his public truth.

Scene 18 - Attainable Felicity

(The Board Room. Day is in the center of a storm of questions. Everyone speaks simultaneously)

SYDNEY
(overlapping) Has the new script been finalized? I literally cannot do anything until there's a new script. Does Ben expect us to design the play as if we're staging the entire book? Because if we are, I have two inns, a chapel, a pier and nine other whaling ships to account for. And I saw a note the other day that we need handspikes. Props designer isn't my forte or in my contract.

ASHLEY
(overlapping) I heard a rumor that the set is changing again. Is that true? If the set is changing I have to have a ground plan so I can reconfigure the plot. And then we can figure out what instruments we need to rent. Joao is asking for a revised budget but I can't possibly give him one until I have a new ground plan. Not to mention the fact that there's no new script yet. Ben hasn't returned any of my emails this week.

NAN
(overlapping) We are out of money. That's the simplest way I know how to put it. I've been putting in eighty hour work weeks. I have no problem with that, but I think my cat has decided that I'm a stranger and is planning on eating me while I sleep. It's not that I don't have confidence that we're headed in the right direction, it's just that this whole thing is going fractal. And we have no money.

JOAO
(overlapping) Do you have a budget? Do you have a budget? Do you have a budget? Do you need a budget? Am I now the prop designer or is that something that comes out of set? Where is Ben? Val has used most of her costume budget already. But this is not her fault. How can she stop buying when everything is changing? Why is everyone yelling?

MICKEY
(overlapping) Ben hasn't reached out to me at all about research packets. A few of the other actors have asked me questions and I don't know if Ben wants me or Faye to answer them. Frankly, I don't feel comfortable without knowing the division of labor. Should I be taking more initiative? If you could have Ben call me at his earliest convenience, I think I can help with all this confusion.

ELIZABETH
(overlapping) I just want everyone to know that I have no idea what's going on. I haven't seen the new script. He hasn't seen a new script. If every-

one can just back off and not assume that I'm Ben's prime minister to the production table, I'd really really appreciate it. I'm just Ben's coffee monkey as far as I'm concerned. Can we at least get some snacks? Nine out of ten doctors agree that snacks make people happy.

JOHN
(overlapping) I'm just trying to do my job. I can't make sound cues for a script that doesn't exist. I've got three external hard drives filled with ocean noises of every possible pitch, tenor and speed and no one has even approached me with the thought of using them. Are we going to save all the sound for tech? I'm in a lot of scenes so I can't be sitting there designing. I have to act. So what's the plan?

VAL
(overlapping) I'm kind of freaking out. Not like "freaking out" freaking out but I can't keeping buying fabric for costumes I'm not going to make. I literally have no budget left. I love you guys but I can't spend my own money on this. Something has to give or at least get settled on. I've got a whole fabric store in the shop now, so I think we need to see if we can make do with what we have.

DAY
(raising her hand) I learned to do this in kindergarten.

(Everyone raises their hand)

DAY
(going down the line) No. Possibly. Switch to wet

food. Somewhere in the building. You'll have to wait for Ben. I'll bring cookies next time. I don't know. I have some expired Valium you're welcome to.

As far as I know, Ben is planning on being at this meeting. I am aware that he's late. I don't have any new information. I don't have a new script. If Ben were here, my guess is that he'd have us go around the table, one at a time, and talk about where we all are.

(BEN and FAYE enter. BEN is carrying one of the heavy boxes he received in Act 2. FAYE has something covered in a silk cloth)

BEN
Good. We have work to do.

(Chaos again)

SYDNEY
(overlapping) Ben, I think we need a prop designer. As far as I'm concerned, I designed a set months ago. Anything that covers the set is decoration and not my purview. Unless we change the concept again. That's what we're all here for. That's what we're all waiting for. We need a solid decision so we can move on. This isn't my only show. I go into tech for Godspell tomorrow.

ASHLEY
(overlapping) If we're still working off the slow fade/slow color change concept, I need to have a serious talk with Joao about load capacity. I don't want the same problem we had during Gravity's Rainbow with the grid crapping out every time

we fire up all the dimmers. I'm already worried about having enough power sources and DMX cable.

NAN

(overlapping) Do we need understudies? I have a short list, but I'm sure you're going to want to be in the room when we bring them in. When was the last time we did a show and an understudy didn't go on. Am I right? We might as well be running a sick ward here. And don't even get me started on paying them. Maybe college students?

JOAO

(overlapping) I had this dream about harpoons. What if each of the characters has a harpoon and they are bent like they are after you stick them into the whales over a long time. And when all the harpoons and spades and shovels and knives are put together, they all make a whale. This is a pretty good dream, yes? I will make all the tools.

MICKEY

(overlapping) Ben, am I still the production dramaturg? I'm not upset about Faye, she's very well-thought-of in her field, but she doesn't do the kind of work that I do in this room. I've had questions from the actors about setting and context, but unless I'm mistaken, I'm very out-of-the-loop, so to speak. Can you please clarify the division of labor between Faye and me?

ELIZABETH

(overlapping) I have absolutely nothing to contribute to this conversation, but I just finished re-reading Moby Dick and it is really funny. Mostly at the beginning when Ishmael and Queequeg have

their buddy comedy. After they get on the Pequod, not so much. Except Stubb. Stubb is hilarious. I want a spin-off starring Stubb. Or, I guess, a prequel since he's dead. Spoiler alert!

JOHN
(overlapping) Have you ever heard the sound of a sperm whale? It sounds like drumming. It's this clicking, tapping language that other whales can hear up to six miles away. They hit this incredibly broad spectrum of frequencies. I've been playing around with them and I'd love to play it for you to see if it's something I should continue to pursue. I love it, but it's your show.

VAL
(overlapping) I'm really good at what I do. Seriously. But I'm only as good as the information I get. I'm only as good as the communication. Every time I get a handle on this show, it changes. It's not fair. It's not right. This company is better than that. We're better than that. Sitting here arguing is a waste of time as far as I'm concerned. Why can't we all just get along?

KAKU
(overlapping) I guess I'm supposed to choreograph something, but I haven't seen any music. John had no idea there was music in the show. Are we making this up as we go along? I like to think of myself as a self-starter, but I can't just make up dances to music that doesn't exist yet. Unless the music comes from the dance? I can do that. I just need some, you know, direction.

PETER
(overlapping) So I'm guessing that the knife

fight between the Spanish Sailor and Daggoo is back in? Or are the whales now being played by actors? Because I can do some pretty wicked harpoon on harpoon action. I call it "Poon-on-poon". Some found-object stuff would be cool, too. A ball of rope dipped in tar could be wicked, like a chain flail. Handspike versus ball of rope? Yeah?

BEN
(putting down his box with a thud) We come bearing gifts. This is the first.

(BEN pulls the cloth off what FAYE is holding to reveal a large origami lotus)

BEN
The Baha'i lotus. This is our new Pequod - the original state of man before corruption, before the Tower of Babel, before confusion.

Moby Dick is a quilt of art forms. We need to use every kind of theatre to tell this story... John, Kaku, look at the song in Chapter 119. We need a big Vaudeville number. Joao, I know how much you love the Town-Ho's story - Chapter 54 needs you and your puppetry. Peter, Midnight, Forecastle ends with a knife fight between the Spanish Sailor and Daggoo. Mickey, you may be the only person on earth who can make the Cetology chapters heartbreaking. Nan, dust off your old Commedia masks - New Bedford is a city of clowns. Elizabeth, The Whiteness of the Whale. The white lotus symbolizes the whole from many. Ashley knows that whiteness is made not from the absence of color but from the commingling of all colors of light.

ASHLEY
Yup.

BEN
It's everything we wanted from the beginning - the Adventure of Memory finding it's ultimate reward in a temple of wisdom in our minds. Let's construct this temple. This set. The platform has nine points, replace the rope-ladders with sails that at the end transform into this flower that closes around Ishmael as he is saved.

JOAO
While he floats in the pool?

BEN
We don't need the pool any more. All we need is this.

NAN
Ben, we are hemorrhaging money. Closing Balm early is double jeopardy: continued expense with no cash flow. We are out of money.

BEN
But we're not out of ideas. We can find money. Ideas like this are priceless. Which brings me to the second gift...

FAYE
(Opening the other box) These are copies of my newest book, "Attainable Felicity - Melville and Baha'i". Read it or don't - I simply want to be able to contribute to this important discussion. If you have any questions, I'll be floating around, trying to stay out of your ways.

MICKEY

I have a question.

FAYE
Of course, I thought you might.

MICKEY
Do you have any primary sources that prove any connection between Melville and Baha'i? Besides your own, of course.

FAYE
Melville visited the Holy Lands in 1857--

MICKEY
Moby Dick was published in 1851--

FAYE
The Bab received his revelation in 1844--

MICKEY
While Melville was still travelling home from Honolulu--

FAYE
When he was inspired to become a writer--

MICKEY
His sisters and father-in-law convinced him to publish--

FAYE
His father-in-law who accompanied him to the Holy Lands--

MICKEY
Which he detested--

FAYE
Because he couldn't find what he was looking for--

MICKEY

Inspiration--

FAYE
Of a sort - the Baha'u'llah--

MICKEY
Whom he had never heard of--

FAYE
Ah, but he stopped in London on his way to Jerusalem--

MICKEY
To visit Nathaniel Hawthorne--

FAYE
Who introduced him to the recently returned Assyriologist, Sir Henry Rawlinson--

MICKEY
There is no proof of this--

FAYE
All of London was in his thrall and he first described Babism--

MICKEY
Then your answer is no - you haven't any primary sources!

(an exhausted pause)

ELIZABETH
Who won?

FAYE
There is no winner or loser. I merely want to contribute to the discussion. You are free to believe either or neither side. Please take one of my books and read it, Mickey. As a gift.

(She hands a book to MICKEY. He takes it)

MICKEY
I cannot wait to read it.

BEN
There, you see? Unity does not mean agreement, it means acceptance.

FAYE
Harmony can be both dissonant and beautiful. The only crime would be silence.

BEN
We need all of these voices to tell our story, as Melville needed all of his crew to tell his.

PETER
What about Amos?

BEN
What about Amos, indeed…

Scene 19 - Sugar Rope

(The lights discover JOHN)

JOHN
Call me Ishmael. Some years ago - never mind how long precisely - having little or no money in my purse and nothing in particular to interest me on shore, I thought I would sail about a little and see the watery part of the world.

(And now we see that he is auditioning for BEN, FAYE, and NAN. A hunched figure in a hoodie sits close by, holding Beary Grant)

BEN
Start again. You're thinking too young. Ishmael isn't the boy who met Queequeg anymore. He isn't even the haunted man who was rescued at sea and roamed the Earth searching for answers. This is the fully digested Ishmael - engaged and engaging. He is practiced, he is perfect. He is ready. For us. Does that make sense to you? Start again.

PETER
Call me Ishmael. Some years ago - never mind

how long precisely--

BEN
Start again. You're threatening me. Ishmael isn't the haunted man who was rescued at sea. And he isn't the boy who met Queequeg. This is the fully digested Ishmael. He is practiced, he is perfect. Start again.

ELIZABETH
Call me--

BEN
No. Next.

AUDITIONER
Hi. My name is Jonas Clay. *(pause)* Call me Ishmael. Some years ago - never mind how long precisely - having little or no money in my purse and nothing in particular to interest me on shore, I thought I would sail about a little and see the watery part of the world. Whenever I feel myself growing grim about the mouth; whenever it is a damp, drizzly November in my soul; whenever I find myself involuntarily pausing before coffin warehouses, and bringing up the rear of every funeral I meet; and especially whenever my hypos get such an upperhand of me, that it requires a strong moral principle to prevent me from deliberately stepping into the street, and methodically knocking people's hats off - then, I account it high time to get to sea as soon as I can.

NAN
That was lovely.

AUD
Thank you.

BEN
Have you ever read Moby Dick?

AUD
I have.

BEN
Once?

AUD
A few times. I was obsessed with Melville for a while.

NAN
And you have no conflicts?

AUD
None.

BEN
Thank you, Jonas. We'll be in touch.

AUD
Thank you. It was nice to meet all of you.

(He exits. ISH enters)

NAN
Isn't he great? He was in a show at Wound Tight Theatre and he blew me away. You're welcome. Should I call his agent?

BEN
No. Start calling your contacts, we're going to need video submissions.

NAN
That's the best we're going to see. How is he wrong? Is he too perfect? He's young but not too young, he's engaging but invisible, he's great

with text. I want to crawl inside his mouth and make a nest.

BEN
I saw him in Look Back in Anger at Wound Tight. His Jimmy was competent, workmanlike. And Arthur hated him. I will not have Arthur enter the theatre with baggage for my Ishmael. Ishmael does not have to earn trust. He is trust.

(The hooded figure stirs)

AMOS
Trust is a sugar rope left in the rain. It is a shadow that flees before the flame. Catch it, fetch it and it's never the same.

BEN
If trust is ephemeral, what is confidence?

AMOS
Confidence? Huh. Confidence is nine-tenths of the law.

BEN
Come with me, Amos. Nan has a lot of work to do, so let's leave her to it.

SCENE 20 - STRIKE

ISH
On the last night of a show, the players skip off to the after party while another group waits in the wings. I speak, of course, of the strike crew: the theatrical Israelites, banished from their homeland until they do the Pharoah's bidding.

(DAY, JOAO, and ISH stand, weapons in hand, looking forlorn as the cast whooshes off)

DAY
Joao, strip her down. We'll start bagging costumes. Do you want props?

ISH
Sure.

DAY
Okay. Go team.

ISH
If you've never spent the night in nearly complete human silence while screw guns whir, piles of wood crash into dumpsters, cables fall from the air...

ASHLEY
Heads!

(VAL, *crossing through with a bag of costumes, is nearly hit by a falling cable*)

VAL
Thank you, heads...

ISH
... as the show you once knew is carted off in box-fulls, bag-fulls and arm-fulls...

(DAY *crosses carrying as much lighting cable as she can*)

DAY
No no, I've got this.

ISH
I highly recommend it.

(JOAO *revs his screw gun*)

ISH
Do you like taking the set down?

JOAO
No.

ISH
No? You look practically giddy.

JOAO
This is a good tool. I like tools. I don't like strike. It reminds me...

ISH
Reminds you of what?

SYDNEY
(*crossing through with a garbage can and several*

tools) Joao, try to save as much hardware as you can.

(JOAO gestures to SYDNEY)

JOAO
It reminds me of the day I left Pico.

ISH
Pico?

JOAO
My home. The money was gone. We knew we weren't coming back. So my father and I took the boats apart, scattered the wood, ripped the sails, took the doors and shutters off the boat house and broke the forge. Then we all took turns throwing the food and rope and harpoons into the sea. Take that, scavengers! No one should get something for free that other men sweat to make. Smash it all, I say, if you don't want it. Make an end of it. Otherwise, you know what happens? Tourists. Like roaches. So no. I don't like strike.

(ASHLEY crosses carrying as much lighting equipment as she can)

ASHLEY
Just think: we get to load in Moby Dick tomorrow! How much Dick can you handle? Better be a lot!

JOAO
So much waste, so much storage, so much decoration. Not enough burning if you ask me. Do you know what part of the whale you can't use?

ISH
No.

JOAO
The butt-hole.

(DAY crosses with a huge bunch of lighting cable)

DAY
A hand?

(JOAO claps as she exits)

JOAO
More things get done when you start with nothing than when you take someone else's trash and and try to fix it. Eat so that you can make. Make so that you can eat. *(gesture)*

ISH
What does *(gesture)* mean?

JOAO
What does it matter? It's just someone else's garbage.

(DAY enters with a heavy garbage bag)

ISH
Can I grab that for you?

DAY
Last one. Why don't you boys head to the party.

ISH
But--

DAY
I'll see you in the morning. Rentals return. Yay. Make sure he doesn't drink too much.

ISH // JOAO
Okay. // I will try.

(DAY exits. JOAO and ISH head towards the door)

JOAO
Now we party.

ISH
Yes! Joao at a party!

JOAO
I'm always at the party.

ISH
I've never seen you there.

JOAO
That's because I'm always in the corner with a woman's *(gesture)* on my face.

(They open the door to the party - it's just PETER and he's really drunk)

PETER
Raise your glasses, ass holes! Tonight, we put to rest one of our own. Balm. In. Gilead. That fucker. He lived a short, violent life, cut down in his prime by a stray bullet. Ashes to asses, dust to dumpster. Anyway, tomorrow, it's back to Big. White. Dick.

(JOAO and ISH help to separate PETER from his drink)

Moby Dick 2 - Funny, Sporty, Gamy, Jesty, etc.

ISH
Chapter 12: The Chase - Day 4

KAKU
Alright everyone, remember: think "Vaudeville". Here we go! A five, six, a five six seven!

(The cast stumbles through a musical number. BEN, FAYE, DAY, ISH and AMOS watch. Beary Grant sits next to AMOS)

THE CAST OF MOBY DICK
Oh! Jolly is the gale,
And a joker is the whale,
A' flourishin' his tale --
Such a funny, sporty, gamy, jesty, joky, hoky-poky lad, is the Ocean, oh!

The scud all a flyin'
That's his flip only a' foamin';
When he stirs in the spicin' --
Such a funny, sporty, gamy, jesty, joky, hoky-poky lad, is the Ocean, oh!

(an Image of ARTHUR appears to BEN)

Um, um, um.
Stop that thunder!
Plenty too much thunder!
What's the use of thunder!
Um, um, um.
We don't want thunder!
We want rum!
Pass a glass of rum!
Um, um, um!

Thunder splits the ships,
But he only smacks his lips,
A tastin' of this flip --
Such a funny, sporty, gamy, jesty, joky, hoky-poky lad, is the Ocean---

BEN and IMAGE OF ARTHUR
It's too literal.

KAKU
Spit take. Like how is it too literal? Do you want to see less hoky-poky?

BEN
This is the storm. I want to see the idea of a storm.

KAKU
You wanted Vaudeville.

BEN
I don't like it. It's too recognizable.

KAKU
So you want a stylized theatrical genre, but not a recognizable one?

BEN
Yes.

KAKU
They're singing about gamy joky rum thunder, what do you want?

BEN
Just the thunder, please Mr. Wada.

KAKU
Just the thunder. Great. Great. I'll bring the thunder.

FAYE
"Unless the season of winter appear, thunder roll, lightning flash, snow and rain fall, hail and frost descend and the intensity of cold execute its command, the season of the soul-refreshing spring would not come."

KAKU
So, thunder?

BEN
Thunder.

(KAKU and JOHN huddle in a corner as SYDNEY and JOAO approach BEN)

Moby Dick 3 - The Cost of Disappointment

ISH
Chapter 20: The Chase - Day 7

SYDNEY
Ben! The Baha'i Lotus thing? I love it. It's beautiful, it's lyrical, it speaks to a dormant shard of my rotting spirituality that I hadn't quaffed in a long time. It seems like something I might have designed in an alternate universe where I feel things for other people.

BEN
I'm glad you like it.

SYDNEY
I like it. I can't build it.

BEN
What do you need?

SYDNEY
We can't use the rope-ladder rigging to hang the sail-petals so that we can transform them into the blossom at the end. In order to accomplish both, I would need the actual sail blossom to be

a separate piece.

(the Image of ARTHUR appeals to BEN)

BEN
I need it to transform - otherwise why did we do it in the first place?

SYDNEY
Okay. So, if we start from the ending blossom, we can position those sails as far out as we can from the beginning in such a way that they can fly together - it just won't be as grand as the original concept.

BEN and the Image of ARTHUR
That is very disappointing.

BEN
How much will disappointment cost?

JOAO
Twenty five hundred.

BEN
Don't stop working on it. We will find the money. Joao, find the money.

JOAO
(gesture)

MOBY DICK 4 - SHEEP

ISH
Chapter 22: The Chase - Day 9

NAN
Ben, did you have a chance to look at the reels from Toronto?

BEN
I did.

NAN
Did you see an Ishmael, she asks hoping to be able to sleep tonight?

BEN
One--

NAN
Yes!

BEN
Two--

NAN
Even better--

BEN
Three--

NAN
What are you doing?

BEN
Four--

NAN
Seriously?

BEN
This is how you count sheep. Repeat after me. One. Two.

NAN
I'm going to find you an Ishmael if I have to call in every actor between the ages of 19 and 39 in the hemisphere.

AMOS
An actor is a jacket.
An Ishmael is a jacket.
An Amos is a jacket.

(The Image of ARTHUR reveals itself to AMOS)

AMOS
I'd like to audition for the part of Amos. Call me Amos! Some weeks ago - never mind how many - having little or no fire in my teeth and a flatscreen TV as a mirror, I took it upon myself to see the watery part of my soul. The great wonder-gates of the flood-world swam open, and wild conceits played me to the surface, and the animals came in two by two, one wide river to cross, the critic and a wrecked canoe, one white mountain to cross.

(Here comes ASHLEY)

Moby Dick 5 - Misunderstanding

ISH
Chapter 56: The Chase - Day 17

ASHLEY
Ben! Can I have a word with you?

BEN
Of course.

ASHLEY
So I just heard that all my color scrollers and moving lights are cut so that we can have the lotus sail thing for Sydney. Just so you know, if I don't have color scrollers and moving lights, we can't have the flexibility we talked about--

BEN
--I'm sure it's just a misunderstanding--

ASHLEY
--because there aren't enough dimmers in the world to accomplish what you wanted unless I can actually change the color and focus of the instruments--

(The Image of ARTHUR appears to BEN. BEN focuses on ARTHUR and is unable to hear ASHLEY anymore. He shakes it off and focuses on ASHLEY again, as the image of ARTHUR exits...)

ASHLEY
And that's why they call them color scrollers and moving lights.

BEN
Joao, I think there was some misunderstanding.

JOAO
Oh?

BEN
Ashley seems to be under the impression that her lighting design has been compromised by budget cuts.

JOAO
Compromised?

BEN
It means to jeopardize--

JOAO
I know what this means.

BEN
I'll let the two of you work it out. We need those color scrollers and moving lights.

JOAO
I'll see what I can do. Day?

Moby Dick 6 - A Row

ISH
Chapter 87: The Chase - Day 29

PETER
Okay, Ben, here's what we got for the Flask/Daggoo fight at the end of Midnight, Forecastle. Mickey, remember, low center of gravity and let me do all the work.

MICKEY *(as DAGGOO)*
Who's afraid of black's afraid of me! I'm quarried out of it!

PETER *(as FLASK/the SPANISH SAILOR)*
Aye, harpooneer, thy race is the undeniable dark side of mankind --

AMOS
A row! A row! A row!

FLASK
-- devilish dark at that. No offence.

DAGGOO
None.

FLASK
What's that I saw? Lightning? No; Daggoo showing his teeth.

DAGGOO
Swallow thine, mannikin!

AMOS
A row! A row! A row!

DAGGOO
White skin, white liver!

FLASK
Knife thee heartily! Big frame, small spirit!

(The Image of ARTHUR exits)

ELIZABETH
Yay! Fight, fight, fight.

PETER
I call this fight "Knife versus Judo". We've got a couple more we can try before the squall breaks it up. We tried putting me on Mickey's shoulders, but--

BEN
(approaching him) Peter, how would a whaler fight? With a dream ballet or *(he pushes PETER)*. You see I think when whalers fight, there's a lot of contact. *(He pushes PETER)*

PETER
Ben--

BEN
Would you like to take a swing at me? See, I think this tension is thrilling. To fight or not to fight.

PETER
I know what you're getting at - that's not safe, Ben.

BEN
If you want to fight, fight.

PETER
It's called stage combat. It's not combat.

BEN
That wasn't combat, that was a dance. I want combat. I want a fight. I want pushing and shoving and "Hey is that a knife" "I can't tell" "I think he's got a knife" "Grab the knife" *(He grabs at PETER's knife)* "Give me the knife!"

PETER
Back off. It's not safe.

BEN
That's it. "Give me the knife."

PETER
I'm not doing this.

BEN
"A row a'low, and a row aloft - gods and men - both brawlers" --

(BEN makes a lunge at PETER who falls and gets up with a horribly bloody nose.)

DAY
Get the first aid kit.

ISH
Got it.

DAY
Peter, don't touch it.

PETER
Fuck! Fuck! Why won't you fucking listen to anyone? This is what happens when you don't fucking listen. I told you it wasn't safe! That's why we don't actually fight in the theatre! This is what happens when you get into a real fight.

DAY
I think it's dislocated.

BEN
Exactly. That's what happens when you get into a real fight.

DAY
Let me see it.

BEN
What are you going to do? Quit?

PETER
Fuck that. Fuck you. *(He pops his nose back into place with a sickening crunch)* Mickey. Let's go choreograph a real fight. *(He exits)*

DAY
Mickey, here's first aid kit and an incident form. See if you can work that into the choreography.

Moby Dick 7 - More New Dancing

ISH
Chapter 92: The Chase - Day 30

KAKU / DAY / SYDNEY / JOAO / ASHLEY
Ben, can I see you?

BEN
Yes, Kaku?

KAKU
New idea. John? Five six seven--

JOHN
Oh! Jolly is the gale,
And a joker is the whale,
A' flourishin' his tale --
Such a funny, sporty, gamy, jesty, joky, hoky-poky lad, is the Ocean, oh!

KAKU
And then imagine they all grab ropes.

(The Image of ARTHUR appears to BEN)

JOHN
The scud all a flyin'

That's his flip only foamin';
When he stirs in the spicin' --
Such a funny, sporty, gamy, jesty, joky, hoky-poky lad, is the Ocean, oh!

KAKU
Then slow-mo and strobe light!

JOHN
Um, um, um.
Stop that thunder!
Plenty too much thunder!
What's the use of thunder!
Um, um, um.
We don't want thunder!
We want rum!
Pass a glass of rum!
Um, um, um!

BEN and the IMAGE OF ARTHUR
The problem is the music.

BEN
It's too "yo ho ho."

JOHN
It's a shanty.

BEN
It's the problem. How much more interesting to use the shanty form and subvert it with, say...

IMAGE OF ARTHUR
Mahler.

BEN
Mahler!

JOHN
Yeah, yeah that's interesting. It's certainly interesting. The only problem I see is that I'm not Mahler and the cast isn't the Vienna fucking Boys Choir.

ELIZABETH
Heh. Fucking boys.

JOHN
I'm serious. Okay? If the music was such a huge issue a month ago, maybe, just maybe, that was the time to let me know. Not after I've spent three weeks working on a huge number with twenty people who kind of sing and kind of dance. Not to mention we have to teach it to the actor playing Ishmael whoever the hell that is!

BEN
So you'll do it?

JOHN
Yes I'll do it. Goddamn it.

KAKU
So more new dancing?

BEN
Yes. More new dancing.

MOBY DICK 8 - DROWNSIDE DOWN

ISH
Chapter 101: The Chase - Day 33

(VAL and NAN enter, with several cast member showing off the Commedia masks. NAN is dressed in her Starbuck costume)

NAN
Ben, we have some things to show you.

BEN
Great. Things. I like things.

NAN
Val?

VAL
Okay. We couldn't afford to ship the actual Commedia masks in from Italy, so Nan and I stayed up the last two nights making these. This is our version of Pantalone. I think it turned out pretty good.

(AMOS sees the Image of Arthur and laughs)

BEN
Amos, what do you think?

AMOS
Upside-down, their downsides drown. Drown-side-down their upsides frown.

BEN
Exactly. They're unusable. Call my man in Florence and have him send thirty leather masks immediately.

NAN
You're using these masks.

FAYE
Trees that yield no fruit have been and will ever be for the fire.

DAY
Ben, we can't afford new masks, much less international overnight shipping of new masks.

BEN
If I hear one more comment about money, I'm going to have Amos scream for me. Do you know the last time I actually took my paycheck from Bad Settlement? Three years. Three years I've donated back to us the fruits of my labors. So don't talk to me about money. Until someone else is willing to make that sacrifice, you have no leg to stand on.

VAL
What about Nan?

BEN
If she wants to donate her paycheck, that's her decision.

VAL
No, her Starbuck costume.

BEN
Have her put it on.

VAL
It is on.

DAY
Val, are you okay?

VAL
I just need to sit down for a moment.

(JOHN *enters in his Tashtego costume*)

JOHN *(as TASH)*
Captain Ahab, that white whale must be the same that some call Moby Dick.

BEN
Does this say "Wampanoag Indian" to anyone?

VAL
I thought we wanted colorful adventure memory?

BEN
Val, if you can't keep up with where the production is heading, ask for help.

VAL
I thought--

BEN
Faye, can you help Val?

VAL
I'm fine--

FAYE
I would be more than happy to help.

VAL
I don't need--

DAY
Val, are you okay?

AMOS
Do you want to talk to Beary?

VAL
No.

FAYE
Thank you, Amos. I'll take her from here. Let's have a good, old-fashioned pow-wow.

(AMOS takes one of the masks and puts it on Beary Grant, then turns Beary Grant upside down)

BEN
Any thing else? Does any one else have a question for me?

ELIZABETH
Ishmael. Question mark?

BEN
Is this a joke to you?

ELIZABETH
No--

BEN
Day, let's call it.

DAY
We've got another couple of hours.

BEN
Everyone go home. You know what you have to do.

DAY
Ben--

BEN
Go home.

(Everyone begins to gather up their belongings and leave)

Scene 21 - The Shotgun

ISH
Chapter 102: The Chase - Day.

DAY
Ben? Can I talk to you?

BEN
Of course.

(DAY hands him her laptop)

DAY
Read this.

(BEN takes it from her)

DAY
I wanted you to know that I'll be sending that before rehearsal tomorrow so we can inform the cast.

BEN
(still reading) You can't.

DAY
You've left me no choice.

BEN
(finishing) You can't.

DAY
We have no money. We have no morale. We have no Ishmael. We have two weeks. Everyone is working their butts off, not because they believe in this anymore... whatever this is now... they're trying to salvage their dignity.

BEN
You know the best work happens when there's something to fight against.

DAY
Why fight it? Fix it. We're moving opening night. We're postponing two weeks and Arthur will be the first to know.

BEN
You can't.

DAY
It's no longer up to you. I'm just letting you know.

BEN
And I'm just reminding you know that if you shoot out that press release, it'll be the last thing you do at Bad Settlement Theatre Company.

DAY
Go ahead. Fire me.

BEN
Fire you? This entire company would simply cease to exist. *(pause)* Oh. You don't know? I forget. For so long, I have been the only thing standing between this company and financial ruin, that I forget what it's like to not stand underneath

the axe of credit cards, loans, landlords, production budgets, ticket projections, reviews... To know what date we have to make what number. You don't want to know. You really don't. It's not pretty, the gaping maw of necessity that could swallow us up opening weekend without batting an eye.

DAY
I want to know. We all want to know. You won't let us know so you can be the one who spends the money.

BEN
Because I'm the one who takes the risks. But you're right. It's up to you now. You want to know how that feels. So decide: which tiger at the gates do you let in? The money lenders? The penny pinchers with their liens and a thousand papercuts? Or the devil we know? The critic with his opinion jaws and ink for teeth? My money is on us. Let's go down swinging. Our talent against the Soul of Opinion.

DAY
You pretend as if all this money spent itself. You lead us here.

BEN
And you followed me. I know precisely where we're going. I have every single one of Arthur's reviews plastered to my walls. Moby Dick isn't my bible, it's my Rosetta Stone. I speak Arthur. I breathe Arthur. I know what he wants. I know what he's after. I know what his reviews are before he even writes them. I know Arthur better than Arthur knows Arthur. He wants a

bold directorial statement, we have that. He wants great performances with non-traditional casting. We have that. He wants an old familiar tale re-imagined to be the conscience of today. We have that.

And if you don't send that, if you trust me, we might just pull this off. What's it going to be? Do we all swim together or walk to the unemployment line on Monday?

FAYE
(having entered stealthily behind DAY) You're the best in the world at this job, Day.

(DAY sighs and clicks delete and sinks back in her chair)

BEN
Thank you, Day. It's good to know there's a little sliver of the old Day left.

(DAY sighs, packs up)

ISH
Can I get you something?

DAY
Coffee. Black. Take your time. I'll be in my office.

(Everyone leaves except BEN, FAYE and AMOS)

Scene 22 - Amherst to Pittsfield

BEN
What if... there is no Ishmael? What if... we start from the moment the Pequod casts off? We give the encyclopedic chapters to appropriate characters and have done with it. What does Ishmael do, precisely, after the Pequod sets sail?

FAYE
Then who survives to tell the tale?

BEN
No one. There are no survivors. Except us, the audience - the witnesses.

FAYE
Then there is no Hope.

AMOS
No Hope. Hope is the thing with feathers--

BEN
That perches in the soul--

AMOS
And sings the tune without words--

FAYE
And never stops – at all –

BEN
And sweetest – in the Gale – is heard –
And sore must be the storm –
That could abash the little Bird
That kept so many warm –

I've heard it in the chillest land –
And on the strangest Sea –
Yet – never – in Extremity,
It asked a crumb – of me.

AMOS
Of me... of me... of me...

FAYE
You are practiced. You are perfect.

BEN
I have to do it. It was me all along.

FAYE
Of course it was.

(FAYE kisses him on the head)

AMOS
(singing them off to the tune of One Wide River)
The audience came in two by two
One white mountain to cross
The critic and a wrecked canoe
One white mountain to cross

One white mountain
And that white mountain is Arthur
Once white mountain
There's one white mountain to cross
(Exeunt)

Scene 23 - One Star

(The entire cast is having a smoke break)

ISH
What was the title?

PETER
It was something like - A Red Letter Moby Dick, Not Remotely.

JOHN
No. It was: "A Red Letter Moby Dick? Not Quite."

PETER
Not Quite. Jesus.

ASHLEY
What a prick.

KAKU
And then he started off all snotty - The act of adapting any masterpiece is...

NAN
First and foremost an act of Ego. He capitalized ego.

ISH
Has everybody read this?

EVERYONE EXCEPT ISH, VAL and ELIZABETH
Yeah/Pretty much/A long time ago.

ELIZABETH
(overlapping) Not me! Tell me more! Tell me more!

PETER
Then he just rips into Ben for a while. He called him an incomplete ego. An imposter.

SYDNEY
Misguided.

JOHN
Right. That's right!

SYDNEY
For years, if anyone told him he was wrong he's say "No, just 'misguided'".

JOHN
And then Arthur got personal, you know when a critic starts talking about themselves. "As a... as a middle-aged man who's seen his share of success and failure, chaos and messes..." how did that go?

SYDNEY
"What makes a masterpiece a masterpiece is taking the personal and making it universal, not taking the universal and insisting to a captive audience that it is personal." Something like that.

NAN
And then he broke it down, like he'd been saving

up insults for years and let 'em loose out of a cage.

KAKU
Hungry, Hungry Hyperboles. What was the thing about Ishmael? That it was easy to cast a young, charming, incomplete man and miss the fact that the Ishmael who tells the story is older, wiser and more complete than all of the characters.

PETER
Then he called the whale the protagonist if the ship was that miserable.

MICKEY
Rubbish. Reductio ad absurdum.

KAKU
What he said.

ASHLEY
Oh god, don't forget the smell-o-vision part.

ISH
Smell-o-vision?

JOHN
Ben had us burn lard under the audience during the try-pots. Had Them - I was eight and my mom wouldn't let me near matches or smoke. *(he absent-mindedly pulls out a cigarette)* Arthur hated it so much, he called it smell-o-vision. Apparently we ruined his favorite shirt.

SYDNEY
And then that last paragraph.

NAN
Oh so painful.

PETER
How did it go?

BEN
(entering in his ISHMAEL costume, AMOS in tow) "Ultimately, I felt nothing for the fates of these ignoble savages. Melville's breathless optimism is replaced with a kind of frenzied sneer - a sure undercut for the tragedy of the finale. No doubt this company will attempt more ambitious projects as it matures and learns to tell its A-team from its B-team. But like Melville's Pequod, it needs to round the Cape of Good Hope and sail through rough seas and quiet winds in order to find it's Season on the Line. But for now, take my advice and just read the book. *(pause)* One Star"

NAN
What are you wearing?

BEN
My costume.

Moby Dick 9 - Opening Night

DAY
Places for the top of act one. Places please for the top of act one.

ISH
Chapter 134: Opening Night. Places, everyone.

DAY
Okay. Let's get this party started. Lights 2 and House to Half. Go. Lights 3 and Sound 1, Go.

(A sound and light effect telling us "Something Is Beginning". BEN starts towards the lights, summons up his words and soul and exits our stage onto the opening night of Moby Dick)

BEN
(off-stage) Call me Ishmael.

(The cast enters into "Moby Dick" in their Commedia masks)

BEN
("on-stage") Some years ago, never mind how long precisely...

Scene 24 - Arthur & Ish

ISH
After the show, the cast and the production team were whisked away for an opening night party on the company dime. I never made it to the party. After I reset the props and helped Day with the performance report, I went to the lounge for one drink. There was no bartender in sight, just one man, older, a bit pensive, nursing a beer in one hand and the program in the other.

ISH
Hello.

ARTHUR
Hi.

ISH
No bartender?

ARTHUR
I served myself.

ISH
(going behind the bar to get a beer) Did you see

the show tonight?

ARTHUR
I did.

ISH
What did you think?

ARTHUR
That is the question, isn't it? Did you work on the show?

ISH
ASM

ARTHUR
I see. Did you enjoy working on the show?

ISH
More or less. It wasn't an easy show, that's for sure. But I really like most of the people who work here.

ARTHUR
All right. No need to talk out of school. How long have you worked here?

ISH
Just this season.

ARTHUR
Hm. I used to love coming here. I know I wasn't supposed to, but I used to look forward to it. At times like this I wonder if it's me who changed or them.

ISH
How long have you been coming to Bad Settlement?

ARTHUR
Every show since their first. And before that, Red Letter. To this day, Star Child Sits is one of my favorite nights in the theatre.

ISH
I wish I could have seen it.

ARTHUR
I wish you could have, as well.

ISH
You sound sad.

ARTHUR
I may actually be angry, I can't tell yet. Something about this show…

ISH
Did you like it?

ARTHUR
That is the question I get asked the most and it is the hardest one to answer.

ISH
Well, what did you think?

ARTHUR
That's the second most asked question.

ISH
Sorry. I'll let you finish up in peace.

ARTHUR
No, it's fine. I'll tell you what I thought. I thought the direction was pompous and desperate, the design was confused, and most of the actors looked like they were giving one hundred and ten percent because they knew the material

was weak.

ISH
Oh--

ARTHUR
It's okay: I've given good reviews to worse.

ISH
Oh. Oh! I didn't--

ARTHUR
It's fine. None taken. Look, there's only three kinds of shows. There are the shows you hate - from the first cue to the final blackout, they're a complete waste of time on every level. They're actually very rare. Almost as rare as the great shows - the shows that keep you fascinated from beginning to end. You know that if one thing were changed, the entire show might fall apart. But ninety-five percent of the shows I see are the third kind. Not great, not terrible. You sit there wondering: how could it have been better? Was it the writing, the direction, the casting? What was good, what was bad? That's why you keep notes - in the end, the play boils down to litany of notions. Most importantly, though, I think: after this show closes, what happens to these people? Do they go on to make something better? Do they learn from this experience? Or is there an inherent laziness to the craft or worse, the insular stench of a rotting corpse. Is there promise amongst the muck worth pointing out?

When I go on record about how I feel about the work, do I play up the promise, knowing a lot of people will go on my recommendation and be disappointed, or do I gently pan it, knowing that I'm practically punishing the company ledger? Its an impossible thing to do right. All I can do is be honest. It's all I've got - honesty. And for those ninety-five percent, I have to choose: which honest thoughts do I print and which do I quelch?

ISH
What about this show? What about Bad Settlement?

ARTHUR
My heart says "give them a pass". The show isn't horrible. Some people will come and afterwards on the dark car ride back to their safe suburban homes, they'll debate which actors they liked, whether the theatre was too cold, whether or not I was correct in my assessment. This company will go on blatantly trying to please me so that they can finally outgrow this once exciting building.

But the little voice in my head, the voice that's nearly never wrong, says: Fuck 'em. Once a company goes down the rabbit hole, the only thing that can save them is reinvention: the kind of wholesale phoenix-from-the-ashes shit that we love to celebrate. If I pan this show, there's a small chance, about this big, that this company will survive. I'm not an idiot. I hear things. I know that there's no money left here. If this show tanks, they're done. But maybe it's time to let go. Maybe it's time to let all this talent back into the pool and see what crawls out. Maybe it's time I finally put a stake in the heart, purge the soul, ashes to ashes, fertilize the soil as it were. Pick your metaphor...

ISH
What will they do?

ARTHUR
What unemployed artists always do: go out into the daylight and say "hello world, what do you need?" Thank you for this chat, you've been very helpful.

(ARTHUR finishes his drink and begins to exit)

ISH
What are you going to write?

ARTHUR
You'll have to wait like everyone else... Good night.

(He exits. ISH pulls out his original, crumpled review of Bad Settlement's Moby Dick. He's had it with him all along)

Review 3 - Thar She Blows

ISH

Thar she blows! Bad Settlement Theatre Company, darts at, misses Moby Dick. By Arthur Williamson.... *(he mercifully skips to the end)* Half a star.

Epilogue

ISH

I know that I'm not the reason this review came out the next day; the reason why no one came to see Moby Dick; the reason Bad Settlement Theatre Company lost the Constellation Motel; the reason this building was condemned; the reason Ben disappeared, at least from theatre; that Day moved south to manage rental properties with her sister; the reason Amos went back to Los Angeles and was mildly successful; the reason Kaku... teaches college; that Elizabeth, Peter, Mickey and Joao...

I drifted, like a coffin on the ocean, from island to island, from profession to obsession, and in that sleep of death, the dreams that came were of a time long since struck like a play in all it's ephemeral glory. The set, destroyed; the lights, returned; the speakers, silent; the actors, gone home. There's only one light still burning. And if you put it out, the ghosts of people past will leak back on, from stage left, up center, the down right vom. From every corner, they creep in, waiting for their turn again.

Lights 708. Go. End of play. Go.

ABOUT THE PLAYWRIGHT

When he was in Fourth Grade, **Shawn Pfautsch** decided he would impress the students in his new school by writing a hilarious parody of popular science fiction films beginning with "Star __". He didn't get any more popular himself, but his short story was published in the school district's student literary collection later that year. This was more impressive to his still-forming ego than to his classmates. He's been fiddling with words ever since.

Several years later, with a degree in Theatre Studies, Playwriting Emphasis, in hand, he moved to the shores of Lake Michigan and helped to found The House Theatre of Chicago, where three of his full-length plays have premiered. Along with his short plays and one-acts, his work has been seen on stages from his base in Chicago to Texas, Florida, Iowa and beyond. What's beyond Iowa? No one really knows...

As an actor and musician, he has been clapped at with The House Theatre of Chicago, The Hypocrites, Steppenwolf Theatre Company, American Repertory Theater, Actors Theatre of Louisville, Dallas Theater Center, Chicago Shakespeare, Lakeside Shakespeare and Michigan Shakespeare. As he was finishing Season on the Line, he was playing Hamlet for Michigan Shakespeare. If any one else out there is playing Hamlet while adapting Moby Dick, please email the author for moral support.

Special thanks to The House, Blair Thomas, David Catlin, Derek Matson and the University of Chicago for the support and especially to the Two Jess's for helping me solve the problems -- in comedy, concept and life.

ABOUT THE HOUSE THEATRE OF CHICAGO

The House is Chicago's premier home for intimate, original works of epic story and stagecraft. Founded and led by Artistic Director Nathan Allen and driven by an interdisciplinary ensemble of Chicago's next generation of great storytellers, The House aims to become a laboratory and platform for the evolution of the American theatre as an inclusive and popular artform.

The House was founded in 2001 by a group of friends to explore connections between Community and Storytelling through a unique theatrical experience. Since becoming eligible in 2004,

The House has been nominated for 60 Joseph Jefferson Awards (19 wins) and became the first recipient of Broadway in Chicago's Emerging Theater Award in 2007. Now in its 13th year of original work, The House continues its mission to unite Chicago in the spirit of Community through amazing feats of Storytelling.

Other Plays From SORDELET INK

Hatfield & McCoy
by Shawn Pfautsch

It Came From Mars
by Joseph Zettelmaier

Ebeneezer - A Christmas Play
by Joseph Zettelmaier

The Count of Monte Cristo
by Christoper M Walsh
adapted from the novel by Alexandre Dumas

A Tale of Two Cities
by Christoper M Walsh
adapted from the novel by Charles Dickens

The Moonstone
by Robert Kauzlaric
adapted from the novel by Wilkie Collins

The Woman In White
by Robert Kauzlaric
adapted from the novel by Wilkie Collins

Eve of Ides
by David Blixt

Printed in Great Britain
by Amazon.co.uk, Ltd.,
Marston Gate.